El Salvador
Testament of Terror

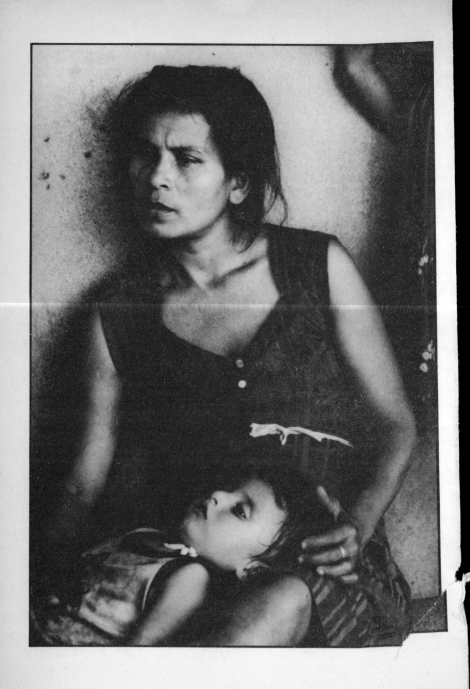

JOE FISH and CRISTINA SGANGA

El Salvador
Testament of Terror

Photographs by Joe Fish

OLIVE
BRANCH
PRESS
An Imprint of Interlink Publishing Group, Inc.
NEW YORK

El Salvador: Testament of Terror was first published by
Zed Books Ltd, 57 Caledonian Road, London N1 9BU, UK, and by
Olive Branch Press, An Imprint of Interlink Publishing Group, Inc.,
99 Seventh Avenue, Brooklyn, New York 11215, USA, in 1988

Cover design by Andrew Corbett.
Cover photographs by Joe Fish/Report Third World.
Typeset by AKM Associates (UK) Ltd, Southall
Printed in the United Kingdom
at The Bath Press, Avon.

British Library Cataloguing in Publication Data

Fish, Joe
 El Salvador: testament of terror.
 1. El Salvador. Political events —— Personal
 observations
 I. Title   II. Sganga, Cristina
 972.84′053′0924

 ISBN 0-86232-740-7
 ISBN 0-86232-741-5 Pbk

Library of Congress Cataloging-in-Publication Data

Fish, Joe.
 EL Salvador: testament of terror.

 Bibliography: p.
 1. El Salvador —— Politics and government —— 1979-
2. Violence —— El Salvador —— History —— 20th century.
3. Human rights —— El Salvador —— History —— 20th century.
I. Sganga, Cristina.   II. Title.
F1488.3.F57   1988   972.84′053.   87-34961

 ISBN 0-940793-18-0
 ISBN 0-940793-19-9

Contents

Authors' Note

To protect the people we have interviewed, it has been decided to alter their names where they appear in this book. Only those names that appear with a surname have not been changed.

Many thanks are due to many people, but especially: to Isabel McClintock, without whom this book would not have been possible; to Matthew Carr, for his reading and comments; to the El Salvador Committee for Human Rights, for their support and assistance throughout; to Claribel Alegría, for the use of her poem *Because I Want Peace,* and to the El Salvador Solidarity Campaign for their kind permission to reproduce the poem here.

The Central American Peace Treaty was proposed while our book was in press. While its implementation by all parties concerned, including the United States, opens up real prospects for peace, there is little indication yet in El Salvador that the government of President Duarte or the forces of the ultra-right intend to abide by its provisions. So long as they do not do so, the war we describe in the pages that follow will continue.

Joe Fish & Cristina Sganga
1987

Because I Want Peace

Because I want peace
and not war
because I don't want to see
hungry children
squalid women
men whose tongues
are silenced
I have to keep on fighting.
Because there are clandestine
cemeteries
and Squadrons of Death
drug-crazed killers
who torture
who maim
who assassinate
I want to keep on fighting.
Because on the peak
of Guazapa
my brothers peer out
from their bunkers
at three battalions
trained in Carolina
and Georgia
I have to keep on fighting.
Because from Huey
helicopters
expert pilots
wipe out villages
with napalm
poison the rivers
and burn the crops
that feed the people
I want to keep on fighting.
Because there are liberated
territories
where people
learn how to read
and the sick are cured
and the fruits of the soil
belong to all
I have to keep on fighting.
Because I want peace
and not war.

Claribel Alegría

PART ONE

El Salvador In Brief

1
Pacifists and Terrorists

At daybreak on a morning at the beginning of January 1986, we awoke on the tarmac of the Pan-American highway in eastern El Salvador after a night of fitful, broken sleep. Through the chill light we watched patrols of heavily armed soldiers pass up and down the convoy of buses in which we were travelling, hardly less intimidating now than they had seemed shrouded in the night. In front of us, blocking our route, a cordon of troops dismissed any approach with brusque hostility.

We were travelling with a group of some 500 Salvadoreans, by now tired, hungry and frightened, and together we assembled in the road to discuss our next move. It was a cross-section of people from every walk of life — a small but representative assembly of the people of El Salvador. There were more women than men, more old than young, as six years of war have ravaged the population of this country; there were many families of the displaced — refugees uprooted from their homes by the war; there were relatives of the "disappeared" and of political prisoners, and also Christians, students, workers, trade unionists, peasant farmers. They were frightened by what they had been through, but they were determined to continue.

These pacifists were marching to demand peace and dialogue in their shattered land.

We were two of about a dozen foreigners who had joined this march in El Salvador. Over the Christmas and New Year period several hundred people from more than 80 nations worldwide set out to traverse Central America from Panama to Mexico in an International Peace March, organised by Norwegian social democrats and sponsored by, among others, Willy Brandt, the West German ex-Chancellor. But the government of El Salvador, like the government of Honduras before it, refused to allow the marchers to enter the country, accusing them of being communists and "Sandinista sympathisers".

In response, groups and individuals inside El Salvador set out themselves to cover the entire route originally projected, and we travelled with them. They wanted to demonstrate their demand for a negotiated solution to the war by a series of meetings and marches in towns all over the country. But they were never to arrive at a single one of their destinations: their Committee for Dialogue and Peace spent more than a week under constant and determined intimidation by the Salvadorean Army and security forces.

We had set out early the previous day from the capital, San Salvador, in a convoy of 12 buses, the people in good spirits, singing and sharing water-melons and oranges. Our first destination should have been San Francisco Gotera, the departmental capital of Morazán province, an area of intense conflict in the north of the country. It is a town which houses some 13,000 displaced people in makeshift camps; many of these families have endured the primitive conditions of the camps for more than five years, and by now they outnumber the local population. The refugees and townspeople of Gotera had prepared to welcome the march, but as they waited well into the night it failed to appear.

As night fell, the soldiers stopped us on the road about eight miles outside the town, and refused to allow us to pass. They held the convoy at a bridge and turned us around, back the way we had come. But this time, as we approached the city of San Miguel just ten miles behind us, the highway was lined with troops — cutting off access to San Miguel itself. On either side of us the streets were dark and empty, sealed off, the soldiers staring in silence. We were taken to the edge of the town and left facing back along the Pan-American highway towards the capital, all other directions cordoned off and all requests to speak to the military authorities denied at gunpoint.

The people spent most of the night watching as the soldiers drove back and forth along the line of buses in small pick-up trucks, which had been adapted with a bench along the middle of the load platform to carry two lines of men, back to back. As they passed, their US-supplied M–16 machine-guns pointed out in every direction like a porcupine's spines.

So it was that when we gathered on the road the following morning at dawn to discuss what to do, everyone was exhausted and scared. The assembly took a vote and decided to continue in the only direction open to us, returning to the capital to denounce in public the treatment we had received. Yet although the caravan set out before 8 a.m. and the distance from San Miguel to San Salvador

The 'Committee for Dialogue and Peace' spent more than a week under constant and determined intimidation by the Salvadorean Army and security forces.

is less than 80 miles, it was a journey that was going to take more than 18 hours to complete.

A series of road-blocks had been prepared for us so that as the march passed through each municipal division or sub-division we were stopped in turn by the army, the police, and the National Guard. The people were taken off the buses and stood in lines under the scorching sun, body-searched and listed, identified and photographed, again and again — each halt taking around two hours and at times coming every fifteen minutes. At one stop, captured guerrillas were brought to try to identify "subversives"; at another point an army helicopter buzzed the convoy, circling low like a menacing gnat.

The marchers formed a delegation which tried on several occasions to request that we should be given a military escort back to the capital, to avoid the need for continuing harassment. But it was precisely this harassment that was intended by the authorities: the delegation was told, cynically, that each municipal jurisdiction is a separate authority and each of the security forces is different from the others and has no jurisdiction over other forces in other areas.

So the intimidation went on, until it culminated in the supposed identification, and arrest, of one of the participants as a "terrorist".

Brigido Sánchez is a 59-year-old peasant farmer from Cuscatlán province, who had been forced to leave his land during the 1970s because of the violence he and his family had faced in the countryside. He had long worked as a Catholic catechist (lay teacher) in the Basic Christian Communities, religious grassroots organisations which have been the target of continuing human rights violations in El Salvador. Sánchez and his family have a history of persecution by the security forces and paramilitary groups because of their religious work: at one point his wife and eight children had been arrested and tortured in detention; his eldest daughter was raped. The family had to flee their home. He was displaced, like so many others, to the slums of San Salvador. We had come to know him well in a small church parish in one of the poor sectors of the capital: a quiet man, he was one of many gentle, but courageous, friends we had made there.

Now, at the end of a day in which the names of every one of the participants on the march had been carefully listed on several occasions, a soldier at yet another road-block claimed to identify Brigido as a terrorist — tantamount to a death sentence in El Salvador. The soldier refused to identify himself or his unit to reporters who were present. His commander later gave a speech

Brigido was taken away by the National Guard, the most feared of the Salvadorean security forces.

lamenting the presence of foreigners, most of whom were journalists, on the march and claimed that they did not understand the situation in El Salvador: "Yankee go home", were his exact words, though the irony seemed to escape him.

Brigido was taken away by the National Guard, the most feared of the Salvadorean security forces; he was held incommunicado for ten days, during which he was tortured and drugged and eventually made to sign a confession he was not allowed to read. The charges against him have never been made clear.

Two weeks after his arrest, Brigido Sánchez was interviewed in Mariona prison on the outskirts of San Salvador by a delegation from the British labour movement, including a Labour MP. They recorded the following testimony of his treatment in the head-quarters of the National Guard, where he was taken at about 9 p.m. on the night of Saturday, 4 January 1986:

> There were two large light bulbs in the room which gave off intense heat. I was kicked and hit on the head. The questions were recorded but I don't remember what they were. I was then made to kneel down continuously until 3 a.m., after which I was taken to a private house — handcuffed.
>
> For six hours I was subjected to death threats and abuse. I was then made to stand up throughout the afternoon, evening and through the night until Monday morning at 8 a.m. During the morning I was punched in the stomach. In the afternoon I was given coffee and a pill which made me lose consciousness at around 3 p.m. The pill made me feel very happy and I had nice dreams, finally waking up on Tuesday at 5 a.m.
>
> Wednesday was calm but on Thursday I was again threatened with death. On Friday I was interrogated from 10 a.m. to 5 p.m., during which I think they interviewed me for television. They kept asking about the reasons for the Peace March and who had planned it. On Saturday and Sunday I was again interrogated for several hours each day. On Tuesday 14 January I was transferrred here to Mariona prison. . . .[1]

Even after these events the marchers tried to follow their original plan. But the same tactics were used to prevent them from reaching every destination, so that for the whole week of their protest they were unable to hold a single meeting outside the capital. One commander, Colonel Ochoa of Chalatenango province, told a priest participating in the march, "You don't have to carry arms to be a terrorist", and showed his open contempt for the people by calling them *malnacidos*: literally "ill-born", crippled, cursed.

2
Christian Democracy and Counterinsurgency

In June 1984 the civilian government of José Napoleón Duarte took office amid a fanfare of optimistic predictions heralding the return of democracy to this tortured Central American republic. But three years on, democracy in El Salvador has more semblance than substance. That a symbolic march to demand peace in the middle of a civil war should so excite the fury of the counterinsurgency state demonstrated clearly to us the extent to which three rounds of elections in four years have failed to shift the real focus of power in El Salvador. To understand why this is so, we had to look behind the elections.

The role of the United States in the region is the key to understanding the present situation: the appearance of democracy in El Salvador is a tactical weapon in the larger war of the Reagan Administration's regional foreign policy in Central America.

The events of 1979 shot Central America from obscurity on to the front pages, and back on the State Department map: a revolution in Nicaragua toppled the 50-year-old Somoza dictatorship, bringing the Sandinistas to power, and in El Salvador the military regime was teetering on the brink, under mounting pressure from all sectors of the society. As in Nicaragua, and also after half a century of dictatorship, the Salvadorean people had united to demand fundamental political and social change.

In El Salvador, a series of military dictatorships had ruled the country continuously since the massacre by the army of over 30,000 peasants in a popular rebellion in 1932. The historical roots of the conflict go back further still, to the seizure of peasant lands for coffee planting in the late 19th Century. This led to the monopoly of wealth, in an agricultural economy, by a tiny elite — the so-called "fourteen families". The elite was, and remains, separated from the overwhelming majority of the Salvadorean people by a vast gulf, of poverty, hunger and suffering; and by an army created to enforce this division by whatever means necessary. It is a picture which can be reproduced in countless impoverished nations throughout Latin America and the Third World.

Traditionally, this structural inequality has excluded all but a small minority from real participation in the country's political process. In practice, a great many of those who have worked to establish a more just society in El Salvador have died in the attempt, whether reformist politicians, priests, peasants or trade unionists. In this way, authentic opposition groups have been forced into clandestine and non-parliamentary activities: they have fought fire with fire.

Unable or unwilling to see the indigenous roots of social unrest in Central America, Washington depicts the revolt of the people against the misery of their lives, against the greed of their rulers and the violent injustice of their societies, as Soviet–Cuban (–Nicaraguan) "aggression". In the United States, the prospect of change in the Central American republics was said to be a threat to US security; in 1979, Jeane Kirkpatrick, later appointed the Reagan Administration's Ambassador to the United Nations, described Nicaragua as "a country whose location gives it a strategic importance out of proportion to its size or strength".[2]

Just weeks after the Reagan Administration took office in 1981, its first significant foreign policy initiative was the publication of a White Paper on El Salvador, allegedly based on captured guerrilla documents and intelligence information, which claimed that:

> over the past year the insurgency in El Salvador has been progressively transformed into another case of indirect armed aggression against a small Third World country by Communist powers acting through Cuba.

The paper further claimed to provide

> definitive evidence of the clandestine military support given by the Soviet Union, Cuba and their Communist allies to Marxist-Leninist guerrillas now fighting to overthrow the established government of El Salvador.

But no real evidence of Soviet or Cuban intervention in El Salvador was ever produced, either in this white paper or on any other occasion. Reports in the US press in which journalists examined the documents on which the paper was based reached the conclusion that:

Unable or unwilling to see the indigenous roots of social unrest in Central America, Washington depicts the revolt of the people against the misery of their lives as Soviet–Cuban (–Nicaraguan) 'aggression'. Worker on a United Brands plantation in Honduras.

The State Department's white paper on El Salvador . . . contains factual errors, misleading statements and unresolved ambiguities . . . . The [*Washington*] *Post*'s inquiry indicates that on several major points, the documents do not support the conclusions drawn from them.[3]

According to another article, in an interview with the *Wall Street Journal* the principal author of the white paper himself described parts of it as "misleading" and "over-embellished", and conceded that it included a number of "mistakes" and examples of "guessing".[4]

Despite the thinness of its rationale for intervention, the white paper provided the necessary justification in Washington for a regional military build-up, which was in fact already under way: the *Wall Street Journal* continued, "Within days, the National Security Council announced it had approved plans to provide the tiny country with $25 million of additional military aid and $40 million of economic assistance".[5]

Central America became a touchstone of the resurgent US right, and a test case for the aggressive US foreign policy of the Reagan years. El Salvador was picked to be the Administration's model success story: it was thought that by supplying the Salvadorean army with quantities of sophisticated military hardware, the rebel movement could be overwhelmed and crushed in its tracks.

But as a recent review of the situation in El Salvador by members of the Jesuit Central American University points out, the situation was not so simple, and this escalation of the conflict has had serious consequences for the country:

From 1979–1985, the United States would invest a total of $1.835 billion in El Salvador. From $9.5 million in 1979, military and economic aid grew to $578.5 million in 1985. These huge sums, and the numbers of US personnel needed to administer them, have transformed the relationship between the two countries. The United States has always exercised tremendous influence over El Salvador's internal affairs. But the word "influence" no longer adequately describes the extent of US control. Since 1981, the United States has operated as a kind of "super-government" in El Salvador.[6]

The Reagan Administration's policy in Central America is based on two overriding goals, which have been pursued in tandem since 1981: to hold back the process of revolutionary change in El Salvador, and to reverse it in Nicaragua. But why these goals should be so all-important is not obvious at first: US investment and commercial interests in the region itself are relatively small-scale, insufficient to account for the Administration's crusading zeal.

The significance of these small and poor countries is, as Jeane Kirkpatrick admitted, their strategic value; but the threat that they pose in practice is that of an example: the alternative model of development that they offer. What is at stake for the United States is its overall position of economic dominance in the hemisphere.

Current US actions fall into a long pattern of intervention which goes back at least to the early 19th Century: in 1823 the Monroe Doctrine declared the hemisphere off-limits to rival European powers; in 1912 President Taft stated his belief that the North Americans were a racially superior people, and said, "One day the whole hemisphere will be ours".[7]

United States economic interests in Latin America as a whole demand that the status quo be maintained: the system that guarantees a compliant government and a cheap workforce for multinational companies should not be threatened, and experiments in independent development should not be tolerated. In 1954, for example, the CIA armed, financed and directed the military overthrow of an elected government in Guatemala — the regime had proposed a limited land reform that would have distributed unused lands owned by a US multinational company. In 1961, the nationalist revolution in Cuba was attacked by counter-revolutionaries trained by US Special Forces and flown in US planes to the Bay of Pigs débâcle — it was only after this that Castro signed his alliance with the Soviet Union. In 1973, the progressive Allende regime in Chile was ousted by General Pinochet in a coup planned and paid for by the CIA.

Jeane Kirkpatrick put the case for this kind of intervention simply enough in 1979, when she wrote, "Traditional authoritarian governments . . . are more compatible with US interests."[8]

And in 1981, launching the Reagan Administration's offensive to "project US power" overseas, then-Secretary of State Alexander Haig proclaimed, "The escalating setbacks to our interests abroad, and the so-called wars of national liberation, are putting in jeopardy our ability to influence world events."[9]

How the Administration proposed to deal with this problem was made clear in October 1983 when the United States invaded the Caribbean island of Grenada, one of the smallest countries in the world. The operation was widely interpreted as a signal that the Reagan Administration was prepared to intervene directly in the internal affairs of states within its "sphere of influence" to maintain its position of regional dominance. Many observers feared that

The threat that they pose in practice is that of an example: the alternative model of development that they offer.

Land reform on a workers' cooperative in Nicaragua.

Nicaragua could be next, and it was also seen as a warning to the rebel movement in El Salvador not to oppose US foreign policy so close to the US mainland itself.

In its Central American "backyard", United States interests override the independence of the backyard-states. The Reagan Administration has sponsored the dirty war of the Contras against the elected Sandinista government in Nicaragua, in spite of a judgement of the World Court at the Hague which in 1986 declared this intervention illegal. Endless US military exercises in neighbouring Honduras have provided the cover under which an overwhelming infrastructure of military bases and facilities has been constructed; Honduras has now been dubbed "the US aircraft carrier in Central America", or "Uncle Sam's brothel" by the less charitable. The neutral country of Costa Rica, which has had no army for almost half a century, now sends its police for security training from US Army Special Forces, the "Green Berets". In El Salvador, counterinsurgency is planned and paid for by Washington.

One event which considerably embarrassed the United States at the end of 1986 gives a clear picture of the extent and the interrelation of Washington's barely covert foreign policy strategies in the region. In October, Nicaraguan forces shot down a C–123 military transport plane over the south of their country. This plane was later revealed to have been carrying supplies from the US to the Contras, a US-proxy army fighting against the Sandinista government from neighbouring Costa Rica and Honduras. The only survivor was a US Vietnam veteran, Eugene Hasenfus, who admitted that he was working for the CIA and had flown ten such supply drops to the Contras in recent months: six of them from Ilopango military airport in El Salvador and four from Honduras. He said that he was paid $3,000 per month for his part in these operations. Documents in his possession, and found on the body of the plane's pilot, who was killed in the crash, were signed by the commander of the Salvadorean air force, the rightist General Juan Bustillo. These identified the men as members of "Group: USA", a unit of United States advisers based at the air force headquarters.[10]

The Reagan Administration's denials of knowledge about these operations were drowned in the revelations of illegal foreign policy operations and Contra slush-funds unleashed by the Iran arms scandal shortly afterwards.

"Traditional authoritarian governments" in Central America, as elsewhere, defend US interests: it is the "threat" of structural social change that is the target of this undeclared war. The Sandinista government in Nicaragua, for example, is objectively more nationalist than Marxist, maintaining a mixed economy with guarantees for private property and a pluralist political system.

Yet superficial changes have been promoted as a necessary ingredient of the counter-revolutionary strategies. In El Salvador, the military defeat of the rebels depends on massive injections of money to the Salvadorean Army. In the early 1980s, the funding was dependent on overcoming Congressional objections to paying the bills of a regime with one of the worst human rights records in the world. When the world's attention focused on the war of national liberation in this country — in which the Archbishop could be assassinated while celebrating mass, for speaking out against murder and injustice — the White House began to look around for a public relations package for its programme.

Elections were seized on as the answer, but in El Salvador's democracy there was no place for even the moderate left to participate. Observing the first round of elections in 1982 on behalf of the British Parliamentary Human Rights Group, Lord Chitnis wrote:

> The election in El Salvador was so fundamentally flawed as to be invalid.... Applied to this country, the choice on offer was that between an impotent and split Conservative Party under the thumb of the military, and a murderous version of the National Front.[11]

In the 1984 presidential elections, the British government's observers reported that:

> We do not agree with the view that representatives of the FDR–FMLN [the political–military opposition coalition] would have been able to participate freely and securely in the election campaign ... had these representatives campaigned openly they would have run a very high risk of being assassinated.[12]

In these circumstances, José Napoleón Duarte, leader of the Christian Democratic Party (PDC), was the obvious candidate for the United States to support. Duarte had the perfect credentials for the international audience he was primarily to convince: he had himself been the victim of political repression by the military dictatorships of the past. Yet the elections which brought him to power were preceded by five years' slaughter of the potential opposition, a period in which 30-50,000 people were murdered. The CIA pumped $1 million into the 1984 presidential campaign; the PDC's electoral success was paid for and enforced by the US, and after the elections the Christian Democrats remained wholly dependent on Washington, both to pay the bills and to keep the right at bay.

Without White House backing the PDC would never have been allowed by the oligarchy to take office. In 1972 a coalition of left-of-centre parties headed by Duarte won the elections only to "lose the count": they were fraudulently and forcibly prevented from taking office by the army, and Duarte ended up in exile. But in the 1980s, it was the successes of the guerrillas in the mountains that won Duarte the blessing of the US Administration.

The Christian Democrats found themselves in a unique historical moment in El Salvador. The party was seen by the United States as the key to a counterinsurgency solution which would enable the Salvadorean military to acquire an overwhelming logistical superiority over the rebel forces. In return for power, Duarte's election victory opened the door to almost unlimited US financial and technical support:

> In the old days, the armed forces ran the country for the benefit of the oligarchy; now, the Christian Democratic Party runs the country for the benefit of the Reagan Administration. . . . Duarte's own role in this strategy is twofold: he opens the door politically for the military to obtain the aid it needs from the United States, and he plays the main *managerial* role in the counterinsurgency project.[13] [their italics]

3
The Price of Power

The Christian Democratic Party itself underwent great changes along this road to proxy power. In the 1970s the party had been a populist, centrist force with its own social base, mainly among workers and middle-class professionals in the capital. It was a moderate alternative to the old right, in a traditionally autocratic society which has never tolerated even moderate opposition: in 1972, Duarte was himself the victim of both torture and exile. But the PDC today bears little relation to the party of the 1970s beyond its name and its leader. In 1980 Duarte returned to El Salvador to preside, as nominal head, over a civilian–military junta. This ruled from December 1980 to May 1982 — the period of greatest violence in the recent history of the country. It was a time when more than 1,000 civilians a month were being slaughtered by government and para-government forces: it was the era in which the death-squads truly ruled the country.[14]

Appalled, liberals within the party and moderate allies quit both the government and the PDC itself. They formed a new party, the Social Christians, and joined with opposition groups in a broad alliance, the Democratic Revolutionary Front (FDR). But in the prevailing climate of political assassination and repression, open opposition was impossible. The FDR was forced to abandon legal political activity altogether when its entire leadership was assassinated at a meeting in 1980, and those who were left went underground and into exile. Duarte, however, stayed: it was at this time that his connection with the military establishment began. An alliance between the PDC and the army was a necessary condition for the party's role in the counterinsurgency project in El Salvador, and thus a prerequisite for the presidency. So it came as no surprise when, in June 1984, the incoming President Duarte reappointed General Vides Casanova as his Minister of Defence, the key power post in the country. The General had been Director of the National

Guard at a time when it had the reputation of being the most brutal of all the country's security forces: the assassins of the four US churchwomen raped and murdered in December 1980 were National Guardsmen under his command.

In government, Duarte became almost completely isolated in the presidential palace: he quickly lost the support of even those sectors of the people whose votes had delivered him into office. At the beginning of 1986, pro-government labour federations, which had signed a "Social Pact" with Duarte in return for votes, moved into public opposition. In February they joined with independent and leftist unions to form a new federation, which immediately took to the streets to demonstrate its opposition to Duarte's conservative economic policies and demanded progress in the stalled process of reaching a negotiated solution to the war.

The "Social Pact" had promised full implementation of an agrarian reform, wage rises and price freezes to lead to economic stabilisation, and negotiations with the armed opposition; none of these conditions has been met. Duarte has been unable to deliver social reforms because his economic policies have favoured business at the expense of the workforce. Measures have been geared to supporting the private sector in line with US regional economic strategies such as the Caribbean Basin Initiative, which stress the creation of "free-trade zones" in which US and foreign companies can take advantage of a cheap workforce, paying minimal taxes to the host government.[15]

The priorities in economic policy have been determined not in San Salvador but in Washington, because the economy is financed by Washington. An austerity package at the beginning of 1986, involving a 50% devaluation of the currency which further fuelled a crippling inflation rate, was imposed under concerted pressure from the US Agency for International Development (USAID) and the International Monetary Fund (IMF). In its analysis, the Jesuit university in San Salvador concludes that:

> By implementing an economic strategy that runs counter to the traditional doctrines of his party, Duarte has accepted a trade-off, opting for power (which is in any case more apparent than real) at the expense of his original programme.[16]

Duarte's budget allocations for social services have been consistently cut — leading not to economic recovery but to increased social unrest. A wave of public-sector strikes at the end of 1985 preceded the launch of the new labour alliance in February 1986. The government response to popular unrest has been renewed repression, and, most significantly, the intensification of death-squad activities from early 1986 on. In May, a series of abductions of workers from Salvadorean human rights organisations, including the Mothers of the Disappeared and the independent Commission for Human Rights, in which detainees were raped and tortured, gave a clear signal that the gloves were off again. Soon after, in June, 16 ecumenical workers, including the Social Secretary of the Catholic Archdiocese, received death threats which gave them eight days to leave the country.

The Duarte Administration can no longer depict itself as the embattled centre, caught between two extremes: instead it has become little more than a "civilised" window-dressing for the traditional repressive security state.

Nowhere is this more clearly visible than in the PDC's role in the conduct of the war. Duarte's election victory was the key that allowed the US to more than double military aid overnight between 1983 and 1984. The proportion of the budget devoted to defence expenditure has increased steadily throughout his Administration, to the point where defence (28.5% in 1986) far outstrips the amounts allocated to health and education combined (22.3% in 1986); the cost of the war as a whole consumes almost half the entire government budget. The US taxpayer is spending more than $2 million daily in El Salvador, with the result that both the overall conduct of the war and the day-to-day course of the fighting are dictated by 'national security interests' as perceived in Washington. In an interview just two weeks after his inauguration, Duarte himself admitted:

> Aid is given under such conditions that its use is really decided by the Americans and not by us. Decisions like how many planes or helicopters we buy, how we spend our money, how many trucks we need, how many bullets and of what calibre, how many pairs of boots and where our priorities should be — all of that ... is decided by the one who gives the money. And all of the money is spent over there. We never even see a penny of it, because everything arrives here already paid for.[17]

His government has been left to manage an open-ended commitment to war which has brought the country to the brink of irreparable destruction.

Out of a total population in El Salvador of around 5.5 million, almost 70,000 non-combatant civilians have so far been assassinated; 7,000 more have "disappeared"; one million are estimated to have fled the country, and some 700,000 are internal refugees,

The Duarte Administration has become little more than a 'civilised'
window-dressing for the traditional repressive security state.
National Guardsmen sent to occupy the workplace during a strike by
public-sector workers.

displaced from their homes by the violence; in addition, there are at present more than 1,000 political prisoners. This means that one-third of the entire population has suffered directly as a result of the policies of this and previous governments in the conduct of the war.[18] A state of siege has been in force for six years (longer than the Constitution itself). Arbitrary arrest and confessions extracted by 'extra-judicial inquisition' (in practice, torture) are legalised in the Penal Code. Sixty per cent of the population live in conditions of poverty or extreme poverty; 60% too are un- or under-employed; 20% of schools lie abandoned. Servicing the external debt accounts for more than half the country's foreign exchange earnings; inflation has compounded since the war began in 1979, and while wage levels are stagnant, the cost of living has tripled in the same period.

Yet the army has grown in strength from 12,000 men in 1979 to 60,000, while the air force has tripled in the three years since Duarte assumed the presidency.[19]

In the counterinsurgency state everything is secondary to the needs of the conflict: in a speech at the end of 1985 Duarte told the Salvadorean Managers Association (AGES), "We are at war . . . and that means that the entire nation is at war. It means gearing the economy to the war. The government's entire effort must be related to the war."[20]

His Defence Minister, General Vides Casanova, had already emphasised the point: "All the resources of the state must be placed at the service of our final victory."[21]

In the meantime, the war has spread ever deeper and wider into the fabric of the society, engulfing more of the country. In 1983, the fighting was basically restricted to the seven eastern departments; today the war is being fought in all of them.

The army is prepared to live with Duarte because his programme is founded on the search for a military victory in the war and resources are allocated accordingly. But that does not mean that it will submit to the constitutional powers of the civilian authorities. The armed forces know that they are the primary guarantor of US policy goals both now and in the future: the war has made them more indispensable than ever. The Army High Command maintains a loyal public profile to Duarte, but their loyalty is fragile. In 1985, for example, commanders in the field refused to honour a Christmas truce which had been negotiated between Duarte and the FMLN by the Archbishop of San Salvador, Monsignor Rivera y Damas: in the departments of Guazapa and Morazán, air force planes bombed villages on Christmas day, while Colonel Ochoa in

Chalatenango said, "We have to forget who is in the government ... and unite to fight marxism."[22]

That military power has grown at Duarte's expense is clear from a study of events. Negotiations for the release of Inés Duarte, the president's daughter kidnapped by the rebels in mid-1985, in exchange for the freedom of 22 political prisoners and 98 wounded guerrilla combatants, highlighted the power of effective veto held by the military over major decisions. The Rector of the Central American University, together with Monsignor Rivera y Damas, acted as mediator in the negotiations, and later described the behind-the-scenes power play:

> The prisoner exchange went ahead despite the military's objections, but only after Duarte had appealed to the ultimate veto power of the United States. Obliged to choose between Duarte and his unconstitutional removal, Washington indicated that it was not yet prepared to tolerate a coup d'etat.[23]

Duarte's command of real power is tightly circumscribed: with the result that, for example, the government's issue of rules of conduct for air force operations has not prevented a continuing campaign of indiscriminate aerial bombing, condemned in public by Archbishop Rivera y Damas. Instructions to the security forces on new procedures for the detention and treatment of prisoners, vaunted as evidence of the democratic government's concern to bolster human rights, are belied by increasing reports of abductions by 'heavily armed men in civilian dress', and testimony by political detainees that torture is routinely used to extract extra-judicial confessions. The government remains unable to account for the 'disappearances' and killings of previous regimes, nor even for those that have taken place during its own term of office: during the kidnapping negotiations, the rebels requested the release of nine people captured by security forces since Duarte assumed power, but the government was unable to provide any information on their whereabouts.

Perhaps most tellingly of all, during the fall-out from the scandal surrounding the downed Contra supply plane and the revelations of its captured US "kicker", Eugene Hasenfus, it emerged that Duarte, though nominally commander-in-chief of the Salvadorean armed forces, was not informed that his air force headquarters was being used as a base for these operations. Washington officials had made the arrangements directly with the Salvadorean military, apparently judging it unnecessary to inform the country's President. Duarte was left deeply embarrassed by the disclosures, his government seemingly caught red-handed interfering in the affairs of a neighbouring state, something he continually accuses the Sandinistas in Nicaragua of doing.[24]

Duarte has accepted a role which leaves him caught in this paradox: he owes his position to the backing of the US and therefore has to accept the war as the main objective of his government — which gives the army *de facto* control over government policy. But the momentum of the war has increased rather than diminished, further reducing the political space in which he can move. The economy is a war economy, whose resources are devoted to destruction instead of development, making it impossible to generate productive capacity or to finance social reform. The public sector is forced to shoulder more of the responsibility of staving off economic collapse — which again increases Duarte's dependence on Washington's purse strings. The price of his survival is to rely more and more on US intervention, but this only serves to tighten the noose around his neck.

Yet the cost of the war is borne mainly by those in the greatest need and who have suffered most.

At the mid-point of his term, Duarte must be said to have failed in his brief. Despite the input of US aid the war has not been won, nor has the balance of forces shifted in the government's favour. The PDC has not been able to reduce the political appeal of the rebels by implementing even limited reforms, and it has not been able to build a centre which could bring into the formal political process those sectors of the society traditionally excluded. In reality, little has changed since the beginning of the decade, beyond the significant fact that the war itself has spread throughout the country and that the massive military escalation has produced meagre tangible results.

Far from advancing national reconciliation, the conflict has been even further polarised under civilian rule, and the hopes of a political opening blocked. At the same time, the war is destroying the country, while for the United States the counterinsurgency project is off-limits and non-negotiable: Lieutenant General Gordon Sumner (Ret.), special adviser to the US Secretary of State, insisted in a March 1985 address to the International Security Council Forum in Washington, "We are not going to negotiate away any of our own interests in this area, or those of any of our friends in Central America. We are not going to negotiate away political power in El Salvador."[25]

So the war goes on. In theory, it should be possible for the Christian Democrats and the rebels to agree a formula of change

The cost of the war is borne mainly by those in the greatest need and who have suffered most.

Desperation is a common sight in the capital and other cities.

and reform which would end once and for all the dominance of the oligarchy, the traditional enemy of both; but the equation is no longer that simple. The ideology of the PDC, and the sympathies of a large number of its supporters, are arguably closer to the position of the rebels than to that of the elite; but the PDC's practical role in the counterinsurgency project has placed it in a different part of the political spectrum. There is some irony in this, in that Duarte's position serves to strengthen his own long-term enemies in the private sector, and the longer he acts out his allotted role the deeper he digs his own grave.

PART TWO

The War Against Civilians

4
Elements of Conflict

In El Salvador, change is not at issue; it is a fact. Revolution takes place first in the mind, as people see their own relationship to the formal apparatus of the state in new terms: as they face history prepared to change it. It is fought not only by guerrillas in the mountains but by a whole people who want to change their lives: a wife oppressed by her husband, a student who does not believe what he is taught, a peasant whose children are hungry, a sacked worker, a mother in mourning. The violence with which their demands are answered in a country like El Salvador is a testament to the strength of their cause, as though it were possible to halt a torrent by shooting it.

The Salvadorean revolution is in this sense at an advanced stage; seven years of struggle have taken its people forward at an accelerated pace. And as we became involved with these people, we came to appreciate the integrity of their conviction; the clarity with which they express their awareness; and the sincerity with which they speak, of themselves, their history, and their future.

A number of visits to El Salvador, throughout the 1980s, have enabled us to know some of these Salvadoreans and learn about their struggle from their own lips; and at the same time we witnessed something of the violence they meet as they face their oppressors. But we also learned that our perceptions and our preconceptions of a battle raging far from home were presumptuous and inadequate, and we found that in our own lives we have much to learn from this conflict and its people.

We were able to interview Salvadoreans of all ages and from every class, recording their analyses, perspectives, opinions, stories; we wanted to document the effect of the war on those who live it, to tell their story from their own point of view, a perspective that does not slot so easily into the east–west/right–wrong formulas of outside analysts.

In January 1986 we spoke with two students at the National University, on a campus scarred by repression. For four years from June 1980 to May 1984, the university was occupied by National Guard troops, who destroyed and looted the buildings, machine-gunned the computer system, stole the dental gold from the medical faculty and hawked typewriters in the street to passers-by. Many buildings are still in ruins, and those in use are mostly bare; students raised funds to buy paint and window panes, but the technical equipment has all been destroyed. Reconstruction costs are estimated at some $25 million (about £17 million). The Duarte government, however, has so far refused to allocate any funds to the university for this.

We had met Victor and Felipe among the peace marchers; the experience of those days had brought all of us close together. Although young, they were calm and confident. It was the strength of the people we met that always impressed us most, that they could make a life filled with danger and with suffering seem so unexceptional, even necessary; and preferable to the security of accepting at face value the world you are brought up into.

Recently [they told us] we had the chance to visit the United States and we were able to meet some Congressmen and Senators. They were very interested in the human rights situation in El Salvador — but they had been tricked. So much that some of them said that in El Salvador the death-squads don't exist any more! What we answered was clear:

"How can you say to us that there are no death-squads when you are sitting here in these fine arm-chairs, and we have just come from El Salvador — burdened with this reality?"

In fact, last year the government used one of these assassination teams to terrorise the university; on July 12 [1985] a list with eleven names was issued, giving the named university teachers and students eight days to leave the country or be executed. Our names [indicating his companion] were both on this list. Three days later they came and dumped four corpses on the steps of the campus to frighten us more; they left the bodies for two hours and then came back to pick them up again. This shows that it was a well-coordinated action. They wanted to scare us off so that we wouldn't continue to demand respect for human rights and autonomy for the university.

One of the reforms announced by Duarte after he assumed office in June 1984 was to disband the intelligence unit of the Treasury Police, reputedly the main information and operations centre for

the death-squads. But the officers concerned were simply transferred to other intelligence bodies: none were prosecuted, and the
intelligence channels were left intact. A year later, in July 1985,
these eleven teachers and students from the National University
were threatened with assassination by the Secret Anti-Communist
Army (ESA) death-squad. They were accused on charges from files
held on them by the Treasury Police unit, proving that the
apparatus of terror and murder was still operating, and still closely
linked to police intelligence.[1]

> In the US we saw an interview with Duarte on TV in which he
> said that the death-squads don't exist any more and that he had
> the situation under control; this is completely false. In our own
> lives we see that they have never ceased to operate, that they
> continue to kill people and to 'disappear' people — we have
> ourselves been shot at in the street. Yes, they exist all right. It is
> one of the demands of the people that the death-squads be
> stopped; and not just that they be stopped, but that they be
> captured and punished for their crimes, because Duarte knows
> perfectly well who they are.

We asked the students why they had not left the country when they
had received threats under these circumstances:

> In no way do we pretend to be martyrs or heroes; as human beings
> we are afraid of death like anyone else. But we decided to stay
> because we believe that we cannot let them drive us out of the
> country so easily. We have to confront the government, and by
> staying we can expose its direct relationship with the death-
> squads. We are here to prove that we are not committing any
> crime, that we are fighting for a cause which is the cause of the
> whole people of El Salvador: to keep alive the right to a free
> education, and to defend this university as the highest organ of
> education and culture in the country. This is the only public
> university in El Salvador and the only one that the children of
> workers or farmers or servants can go to — most of us who study
> here are from working-class families. We are both from working-
> class families.
>   So we are not going to allow them to demoralise us; we
> have taken the responsibility to stay and to continue our work;
> and we cannot betray the thousands who have shed their blood
> before us.
>   We don't need any more exiles in our country; what we need is
> a free country where we can live in peace. And if our own blood is

the price we have to pay to free our people, well, we are prepared to pay it.

These were not empty words. One month after this interview we learned that one of these friends had been arrested, and was being detained by the National Police.

At the time, it was hard to grasp that our conversation was not as natural as a group of friends discussing views over a full ashtray. One of the questions we especially wanted to ask was how Felipe and Victor themselves saw the conflict in their country — what are the roots of the conflict?

Central America has always been characterised by repressive governments, exploiting the weakest and neediest of the people. In El Salvador, a popular movement began almost at the beginning of the century, when people realised their exploitation and saw that instead of getting better it was getting worse. So they began to form the first unions and to fight for better conditions. The movement they built at this time was very strong, so strong that it culminated in an uprising of the people. But it was brutally suppressed — the government massacred more than 30,000 Salvadoreans [in 1932].

From that day to this only the faces have changed; the repression and the suffering have remained. But people continued to organise, despite the repression; especially in the countryside where peasant leagues and Christian federations tried to defend land rights; and in the cities public employees and teachers established their own unions.

Some of those involved saw that the only response they got from the government was murder, more repression and more exploitation; so they decided to take up arms. But the popular organisations continued to fight for better salaries and decent living conditions, and money for health services and education. The government, as it had 50 years before, just answered with violence.

By the 1970s, a popular alliance brought together all the different sectors: trade unions, student groups, teachers, peasants, shanty-town dwellers, Christian federations and market women — the whole people were united to demand an end to the dictatorship. But as in 1972, the military cynically manipulated the 1977 elections and refused to let the winning opposition candidate take power: they simply said, the opposition is not going to win, they cannot take the Presidency, so the candidate of the military and the oligarchy is going to win. The people took to the streets to protest and occupied the Plaza Libertad [in the centre of San Salvador]; after six days the government sent in troops who slaughtered more than 300 people for demanding that the results of the elections be respected.

In 1979 popular pressure was so strong that the military organised a *coup d'etat* and invited some of the popular leaders to join a junta — but it didn't even last two months. The army continued its programme of indiscriminate assassination. The civilian leaders had agreed to participate in the government because they thought that they could reach a political solution to the country's problems, to end the violence. But they soon saw what was really going on and they quit the government — only the Christian Democrats stayed, and within the Christian Democrats the most progressive sector left the party. The group headed by Duarte was left alone, and it was at this time that the Christian Democrats became clearly identified with the military and the oligarchy.

In October 1979, the military had decided to strike the first blow in the civil war which had by then become unavoidable. Just three months before, they had seen a broad-based popular coalition of opposition groups overthrow the Somoza regime in neighbouring Nicaragua, and had not failed to draw the lesson. The coup, presented as a reformist initiative of junior ranking officers, was a pre-emptive measure designed to save the old order just as it was about to be overthrown from below by the popular organisations which would now become the targets of intensified repression. Civilians were appointed to sit with the generals on a new junta, but they had no real power. Within a week of the October coup more than 100 strikers and demonstrators had been shot dead in cold blood by security forces in San Salvador alone. In the countryside, peasants who demanded the implementation of a new minimum wage decreed by the civilian–military junta were answered by violence: in one incident on 18 December 1979 troops backed by armoured cars and helicopters attacked a group of protesters on a coffee plantation and left at least 100 workers dead. On the capital's streets and vacant lots the mutilated bodies of trade unionists detained in earlier raids began to appear daily at dawn, outnumbering those of the previous day. The death-toll, monitored by the human rights office of the Catholic Church, exceeded 1,000 people per month.

At the beginning of January 1980, only ten weeks after the coup, the civilians resigned en masse from the government, paving the way for a new junta on which only the Christian Democratic Party (PDC) sat with the military. Then in March, Héctor Dada, leader of the PDC during Duarte's exile, and six other PDC members of the government resigned not only from the government but from the party itself, taking much of the rank and file with them. Dada, naming Duarte, declared that those leaders of the party who continued to collaborate with the military regime did so in defiance of the party's membership.

Within three years of the coup, the death toll had exceeded the 30,000 killed in 1932 and included the Archbishop of El Salvador, Monsignor Oscar Romero.

Archbishop Romero died on 24 March 1980 from a single rifle-shot through the heart while celebrating mass; the day before, he had delivered a homily in which he urged the lower-ranking soldiers in the army and security forces not to obey orders to torture and to murder; from so influential a figure this was dangerous talk, and he went even further, adding:

> . . . in a country such as ours where injustice reigns, conflict is inevitable . . . when a dictatorship violates human rights and attacks the common good of the nation, when it becomes insupportable and all channels of dialogue, understanding and rationality are closed, when this occurs, the Church speaks of the legitimate right to insurrectional violence.[2]

The assassination of the Archbishop was the event which clearly and irreversibly announced the outbreak of a full-scale civil war in El Salvador. Since the October coup the army had concentrated on eradicating all possible challenges to its power, however moderate, almost before the popular movement realised what the true situation was. Romero's murder was an unmistakable signal of the lengths to which the oligarchy was prepared to go to maintain itself. Four days later, a crowd of 100,000 mourners who had gathered in the Cathedral square for the Archbishop's funeral fled as machine-gun fire rained down indiscriminately upon them. Despite official government denials, a joint communiqué signed by clergymen and bishops from all over the world who were present at the funeral stated unequivocally that the shooting had come from the second floor of the National Palace opposite.

The immediate aftermath of these events was the final unification of opposition, both political and military, to the regime. Social Christians — those who had left the PDC in protest — and Social Democrats united with independent labour unions and popular organisations to form a broad political opposition, the

The assassination of the Archbishop was the event which clearly and irreversibly announced the outbreak of a full-scale civil war in El Salvador.

The tomb of Monsignor Romero in San Salvador Cathedral.

Democratic Revolutionary Front (FDR). At the same time, the armed opposition established a unified command structure to coordinate guerrilla operations, and in October 1980 formed a single guerrilla coalition, the Farabundo Martí National Liberation Front (FMLN). Within the country, the climate was tense and the atmosphere dominated by fear and death: by the end of the year some 10,000 civilians had been murdered by the government, and in 1981, Duarte's only full year as President before the 1984 elections, at least 13,500 more died as a result of the terrorism of state security forces.[3]

Victor and Felipe described to us what it was like to live in El Salvador during these years:

> The government surrounded whole areas and took away the young people to kill them, dumping the corpses the following day. Many people had to leave the cities to escape assassination, and many decided to join the armed struggle; others fled abroad and those who could not escape were killed. A few of us managed to stay in the cities, sleeping in one place one night and somewhere else the next, and in this way we were able to avoid capture and have survived up until now. The university suffered greatly: from 1980 to 1984 715 students were murdered, more than 300 "disappeared" and many others were captured.

Any non-violent political option to bring about change was buried in November 1980, when uniformed army and police troops surrounded a school in which leaders of the FDR were holding a conference. Plain-clothesmen entered the building and abducted six of the party's top leadership, including FDR president Enrique Álvarez Córdoba. The following morning the bodies of all six were found riddled with bullets and slashed with *machete*-wounds. Surviving FDR members were forced underground or into exile, abandoning legal political activity inside the country. The FDR joined the armed opposition to form the FDR–FMLN political–military coalition; and by now the whole of the popular opposition recognised the need to fight for revolutionary change. No other alternative was left open; the legal means to bring about a reorganisation of wealth and power were cut off.

To understand the war it is essential to see the social context that makes transition in El Salvador an imperative that cannot be wished away. We put this question to a teacher from the capital whom we met in the offices of his union, one of the strongest in the country. There was a small course training popular educators, voluntary literacy teachers organised by the union, who work in the deprived rural areas of the country. Ramón was taking the course, a man of about 40, very fit, and direct; as he spoke, he was unemotional, almost clinical, as though he meant to make sure that we did not miss the basic points we had asked him to make: in El Salvador, more than 330 teachers have been murdered, the where-abouts of another 78 are unknown, many more are in exile and more than 5,000 are unemployed — while over one-fifth of the country's schools lie abandoned. Ironically, the only teacher-training college in El Salvador is currently occupied by the US-trained elite counter-insurgency battalion, the Atlacatl, which uses the college as its barracks.

Our fundamental problem [Ramón explained] is that a small minority owns and enjoys all the wealth of the land, while an overwhelming majority lives in conditions of absolute misery. To the rich in this country the people are no more than beasts of burden, to be worked until the last drop of sweat is extracted — they are not human beings who deserve a decent life. This is why huge sums of money are spent to maintain the armed forces, the police forces, the security forces, the paramilitary forces, the intelligence forces and the death-squads — while the budget for health is totally insufficient to meet the needs of the people.

For example, illiteracy in El Salvador exists precisely because of this injustice. Here, we grow agricultural produce for export abroad — coffee, sugar and cotton. The raw material is produced cheaply and sent for processing in the industrial world, and for this the plants must be cultivated and harvested; well, it is the peasant who does this work. So those who own the production and the wealth must keep the peasant — and all his generations to follow — permanently a peasant, to maintain the system that gives them their wealth. The only way to guarantee this is to keep him illiterate, and this is why 84% of the peasants in El Salvador are illiterate — nationwide, 65% of the whole population are illiterate.

In recent years, the education budget, like the health budget, has been cut back even further to pay the increased costs of the war, so that in this way the people are even paying for the war that is waged against them.

The Salvadorean oligarchy is utterly conservative; its privileges have been so great that they are unwilling to give up any part of them, however small — but sooner or later here things are going to change.

In El Salvador, to take steps toward achieving this transition can

"I have felt in my own flesh the injustice that exists in this society. It is this personal experience that really makes a person aware".
Demonstrators hide their identities on a protest march.

be tantamount to signing your own death-warrant; in Mexico City we spoke to Reynaldo, a Salvadorean worker now living in exile, who explained to us how he had come to be involved in a struggle that almost cost him his life:

I am 28 years old: during my childhood and youth I saw my parents suffer because of the injustices of my country. My parents were workers, my father a carpenter and my mother a baker; as a child I witnessed situations like when they were sacked and unable to get any kind of compensation. At school I began to understand this, and I started to develop a political awareness and then to participate in student councils. Later, when I in turn became a worker, I joined the union and by this time I had a clear understanding. I was a technician in a hydro-electric plant where the union was very strong.

One thing that stands out clearly for me is that repression has played a fundamental part in developing my political under-standing; I was always aware of the repression, from seeing the callousness of the boss, to finding friends, fellow-workers, neighbours and fellow-students, murdered or imprisoned, tortured. This was something that could not be ignored. And like all Salvadoreans involved in union activity, I too experienced this repression.

There was a labour dispute in the plant where I worked, and we went on strike to demand the reinstatement of sacked workers, the payment of arrears of salary and the release of other union members who had been abducted: 98% of the plant's workers took part in the strike. After 24 hours, at noon, government security forces stormed the plant and abducted all the workers. I was one of those arrested. We were taken to the barracks of the National Guard, where we were tortured: we were not allowed to sleep, we were awoken with a knife held to the throat or with a gun-barrel in the mouth; they threw tear-gas into the cell where some 40 of us were shut up in a space about four yards by eight; they beat us and interrogated us for three weeks, and during this time we were not allowed to communicate with anybody. From there we were taken to the jail in San Salvador. The security forces arrived at the jail and started to beat all the political prisoners, especially us because we were members of a union; we were beaten with rifle-butts and they used the *capucha* on two of my friends [the *capucha* is a form of torture in which an airtight hood filled with lime is held over the head of the victim, choking him with extreme pain]. They broke the ribs of two others and cracked the skull of one.

I feel that with my own blood I have tasted the life of an activist who tries to work for the rights of fellow-workers in El Salvador, and I have felt in my own flesh the injustice that exists in this society. It is this personal experience that really makes a person aware. I spent four years and four days in prison; yet I believe that when a fight is just, as ours is, then you have to go on with it. Our fight is just because of the conditions that have existed in this country for the last 50 years, and even longer.

I was released in October 1984 and I remained at first in San Salvador; but I had to flee because I received threats from the death-squads, saying that I had 30 days to leave the country or they would kill any member of my family. That is why I had to leave.

5
Land and Liberation

The roots of the conflict, and the type of society the people are trying to construct, can be seen most clearly in the zones that have been controlled by the rebels. The people's experience during the six years that the government — and the landowners — have been excluded from these areas of the Salvadorean countryside amounts to an experiment in self-determination: an agrarian reform at grassroots level that projects a scheme of development designed by the people themselves to fulfil their own potential.

The zones of guerrilla control are areas traditionally isolated and ignored in the social structure of the country. The land is unsuitable for large-scale coffee cultivation and so has had little value in the development of the agro-export economy. These areas on and around the slopes of inhospitable volcanoes are made up of land characterised by slash-and-burn subsistence agriculture, whose soil has become exhausted by over-use and lack of investment. They are the regions of bleakest poverty in all El Salvador: the provinces of Morazán and Chalatenango, along the northern border with Honduras; parts of Cabañas sandwiched between them; Cuscatlán, dominated by the Guazapa volcano in the centre of the country and overlooking the capital; San Vicente and San Miguel dotted with mountains towards the east; and Usulután on the Pacific coast.

The people who live in these areas are families descended from migrants who were forced off their own plots in the lowlands and central highlands to make way for the expansion of cash-crops: after coffee in the 19th Century came cotton in the 1940s, and sugar in the 1960s. The marginal lands that were left to the peasants were barely able to support the cultivation of basic foods — corn and beans. Traditionally, their lives have been characterised by the most severe deprivation, lacking not only an adequate diet but almost any type of social infrastructure or basic amenities: schools,

Traditionally, the peasants' lives have been characterised by the most severe deprivation.

hospitals, roads, water, electricity, sewage, and so on were virtually unknown. For this reason, all the statistics for deprivation in El Salvador — malnutrition, illiteracy, disease, infant mortality — are disproportionately aggravated when applied to these rural areas, which came to be the rebels' strongest bases of support in the 1980s.

On even this inhospitable land population pressure increased throughout the 20th Century, and the majority of the peasant families were no longer able to support their subsistence needs solely from what they could produce on their small plots. Changes in land tenure and sub-division or over-exploitation of tiny family units combined to force the peasants off the land again. In particular, the trend was towards families renting rather than owning their land, and paying the landlord by money rent rather than in kind — often demanded in advance. The landless population grew from 12% in 1960 to 40% in 1975, by 1980 reaching an estimated 60%.[4] Life in the countryside became harder, and the peasants had to rely increasingly on seasonal labour to earn money to pay rent — an annual migration to the commercial estates where working conditions are primitive and wages minimal.

In areas under government control, these conditions can be seen clearly in El Salvador today. Whole families still go down to the plantations with the onset of the dry season, from November to March, to perform back-breaking manual labour in conditions that leave them sick from malnutrition and exposure to chemicals and crop-fumigation. They are barely able to make enough money to pay off debts they have accumulated just to survive at subsistence level. Worse still, the plantation workers are temporary employees who have no contract with their employers, nor any right to form unions to negotiate better wages or improved conditions of work. The official rural minimum wage at the time of writing is eight *colones* per day (about £1 in Britain or just over US$1.50) but many employers do not respect even this, since work is scarcer than workers.

Historically, as the peasants' situation became more desperate, several factors combined to mobilise this traditionally passive and victimised class. First, in the 1960s, was the change in the attitude of the Catholic Church. At the Second Vatican Council of 1964, and at the conference of Latin American bishops at Medellín in 1968, the Church reassessed its traditional role and adopted what became known as its 'preferential option for the poor'. This involved a commitment to working with the people to improve their material conditions of life and to end the exploitation and misery they suffered.

The Medellín documents openly denounced the poverty and brutality of the relations of production in Latin America. In practical terms, this change meant that the work of the priests would aim to encourage the peasants to organise themselves, in Basic Christian Communities. Through the Basic Communities they would discuss and seek to understand the injustice of their lives. This "theology of liberation" was a process through which many people came to understand the political reasons for their suffering for the first time and began to think about how to bring that suffering to an end. It was a process of "consciousness raising" which in fact worked both ways — as peasants became politicised, many priests became directly involved in the peasants' problems and were themselves radicalised.[5]

These forces were eventually to mature into an organised movement demanding fundamental social changes — and prepared to fight to win them. The Basic Communities were an important stage in which people learned to analyse their problems and also learned the value of working together to confront their situation. In the 1970s many of these activists went on to build the first organised peasant union and sought to answer the thorny question: how were the people to liberate themselves, and what kind of liberation would it be?

Change was, and still is, the critical demand of the people, and so long as it was not achieved the pressure built to force ever more radical answers. The peasants formed and ran their own union and learned to challenge the state on a practical and political level. At the same time they began to collaborate with other sectors: labour unions and students in the cities who were similarly struggling for change.

The peasants' awareness and growing strength led directly to the other major factor in their political development: repression. Far from resolving the demands that were now being expressed, the government launched a programme of violence designed to stifle the peasants' voice. Many of the priests who had helped to organise the people also became targets of official violence, culminating in the assassination of El Salvador's most famous martyr, Archbishop Oscar Romero, in 1980. In 1975 the first of the death-squads appeared, the FALANGE, calling for a return to the methods of 1932 (when more than 30,000 peasants were massacred); in March 1977 the first priest to be murdered was Father Rutilio Grande, who had worked with communities in the Aguilares region around the Guazapa volcano; and the same year another death-squad, the White Warriors Union, circulated handbills announcing, "Be a

Patriot, Kill a Priest". In just four months between February and May of 1977, 17 priests were expelled or forced to flee the country, four imprisoned and tortured, and six killed.[6]

The repression was coordinated through ORDEN (Spanish for "Order" and an acronym for National Democratic Organisation), a nationwide paramilitary organisation which had been set up in the 1960s with advice and funds from US Army Special Forces (the "Green Berets"). Membership of ORDEN was overwhelmingly drawn from the local peasant population, and its ideology was based on a selective patronage, favouring a limited number of adherents in order to strike fear into the community and prevent real initiatives for reform taking root among the people. ORDEN established a comprehensive network of agents and informants based in every community throughout the countryside, by drawing on ex-army conscripts and offering certain privileges to its members in exchange for denunciations and strong-arm tactics.[7] In practice, they were dirty-warfare gangs along the lines of the European fascist movements of the 1930s — with strong kinship ties and a tendency to settle private scores shielded by the state.

As the situation in the countryside became more combative towards the end of the 1970s, the tactics used by ORDEN became correspondingly more brutal. In one of the church refugee centres we visited in San Salvador we asked Enrique, a peasant farmer of about 35 who looked like a haggard 50 and was now displaced from his home in Guazapa, what conditions in the countryside were like during these years.

In the countryside the problem has been that the landowners are unwilling to pay the workers more or to improve the conditions of work. We were afraid to make any demands because if we opened our mouths we were accused of being subversives, so we just had to bear our tasks in silence.

We formed an organisation which helped us and made us feel stronger. Then the death-squads began to appear, and they took away many of the workers who were active in the union — they beat them up and killed some of them. There were many deaths, as they took the people from their houses at night and dumped the bodies in the streets — so many that the road from Aguilares to Suchitoto [in Guazapa] was turned into a cemetery; even today we sometimes find the bones of the corpses they dumped.

The death-squads were formed from the same peasant population as their victims — they were members of what was called ORDEN. Those that had the guts to kill were put into ORDEN. It was an organisation that they said was for defending the interests of the peasants, but we could see that it was not our interests but the interests of the landowners that they were protecting.

Neither the spread of ORDEN throughout the countryside nor its brutality could prevent the growth of an independent and radical peasant rebellion, since it had no solutions to offer to the underlying problems which provoked unrest. The violence did not crush the peasant movement: instead of destroying their organisation its effect was further to radicalise the peasants, and to strengthen their resolve to fight. The country was ready to explode: armed revolutionary groups that had emerged in the 1970s had begun to establish bases in the rural areas by the middle of the decade, and to collaborate with the local population; at the same time, the peasants' union had joined with other groups from the cities to form a unified popular opposition to the military regime.

By 1978, civil war had almost erupted as ORDEN tactics turned to wholesale terror. In response, the peasants organised self-defence against ORDEN and undertook land invasions to press their economic demands. In the cities too, the pressure was about to burst and the October coup of 1979, which brought civilians into a government junta but denied them any real power, served only to postpone the moment. On 22 January 1980 a quarter of a million people marched in the capital for what was to be the last mass demonstration by the popular organisations for many years: more than 50 people died when government forces attacked the march. It was against this background that Archbishop Romero spoke of "the legitimate right to insurrectional violence" — and against this background that he was murdered, the single event which finally proved that the regime could not be dealt with by any means other than armed insurrection.

The war broke out in earnest at the beginning of 1981. As the country quickly divided into areas under the control of the army or of the armed opposition, the rebel groups established rearguard bases in many rural areas, which covered a quarter of the national territory by 1984. The local people in these areas were able to take control over their own lives for the first time in their history. This allowed the peasant organisations to establish fully fledged elected local councils to take charge of the day-to-day administration of the zones, an unprecedented experiment in village-level democracy. The significance of this was explained to us by a peasant woman

The local population were able to take control over their own lives for the first time in their history.

from the department of San Vicente; dressed in practical work-clothes, María Rosario must have been barely 16 years old when civil war changed her life:

> Before, the zone was full of coffee plantations and there were fruit trees, but we were forbidden to eat the fruit; the landowners made us work the land but we were not allowed to eat any of its produce — even if the fruit had fallen to the ground we had to go hungry. We were not organised then, but later with our experience of the repression we saw the need to work together. So we started to organise the work collectively, and we also organised schools since almost 90% of us were illiterate. And the rest, perhaps they had gone to school and could write a few words and their name, but it would take them a whole day to fill a page. So we had schools — in the day for children and at night for adults. In '82/'83 we could do this easily, but later it was more difficult because of the intensification of the bombings, but we still continue to do these things.

The government forces are able to penetrate these zones only in major military operations, during which the people flee into the hills, to return when the army has left. Yet despite the constant danger of army attacks, those who live in these rural areas will not willingly leave their homes for an uncertain future in city slums. The following testimony was taken by Archbishop Rivera y Damas during a visit to Guazapa in October 1985:

> An old woman had nowhere to hide but in a ditch. When the soldiers came they told her to get out. She told them, 'I'm not going anywhere; no, I was born here and here I'm going to die. Here is where I have my home and here is where I'm going to die.' The woman was more than 70 years old, and they murdered her right there. It wasn't enough just to shoot her, they took her out and threw a burning acid over her and left her there. We who live in these places have seen things that we never should have seen, things we never thought to see.[8]

A Catholic priest in San Salvador who had accompanied Monsignor Rivera in Guazapa, and later in Chalatenango, described to us what they had seen on this trip:

> The conditions in Chalatenango are terrible, and they are even worse in Guazapa. What we saw in Guazapa was shocking: there wasn't a house left standing, the people sleep amongst the trees, wherever they can — they make little huts to keep the rain off, or

else they sleep in hammocks and cover themselves with plastic sheeting . . . .

The conditions are also terrible because the people cannot grow enough food — it is a place where there have been so many military operations that there has always been an attack which destroyed everything . . . .

Guazapa has a population that is truly heroic.

Part of the reason why the people will not leave is that they are tied to their land by a complex spiritual relationship rooted in their Indian cultural heritage, and this, coupled with economic factors, makes it hard to abandon the only life they know. The priest explained the significance of the land to these people:

One important thing to understand is the value that all these people place on the land, the land as mother, as the source of life, as the point at which their lives are fixed; so that to take them away from the land is a crime. For the people to lose all they have and know, their house and their plot of land that they have worked and suffered greatly to get, to lose this is to lose everything. They don't have money; they don't know what will happen to them, or whether they can find work. The work that they can get on the harvests lasts only two months and they have to survive the other ten; if they don't have their *milpa* [cornfield] they don't have anything . . . .

Even more significant are the social changes that have been achieved in these isolated communities. Even today, in the face of war, they run health and education programmes and organise food production for the whole community. What people lacked in experience they have made up for in determination, and they have organised structures appropriate for their real and urgent needs. They divide responsibilities and benefits among the communities by discussion and agreement, and assign tasks within each community by electing leaders in charge of the various duties, not experts or politicians, but people who have some kind of experience which better qualifies them for the work.

Self-defence, involving digging bomb-shelters and planning routes of escape, as well as popular militias to keep watch for the army's approach, or to make sure that everyone keeps up during the flight from a military operation, are also organised. The posts are rotated regularly to enable as many people as possible to take on the responsibilities, learning to organise the work of running the society, and preparing to take a part in the new society they hope to achieve for the whole country. Clara, a young woman who works as a medical auxiliary with communities in rebel-held territories in San Vicente, where the civilian population has been decimated by military drives, explained how the people have managed to take control over their own lives:

> We organised *Poderes Populares* [local popular authorities] so that we could participate in the running of the community. This was difficult because we all had a lot to learn; we said we had so many problems because we came from a system that was so unjust. But we decided that we should share out these failings and maybe after a couple of generations we would be able to build a better life.
>
> Every January 22 we have elections; we chose that date because on January 22 there was a massacre in San Salvador in 1980. All who live in the zone can vote, from the age of 14 up; it is like this because young people are such a large part of the community — since with the repression the average age now is about 30 — and we can't leave these people out of decisions when they have lost their parents and families and have suffered so much. They are adults already; and also they work and produce like all of us.
>
> So in this way we have our own government to organise everything we need. People are learning that we can all participate in the society, and that everyone can do something.

The structures of the popular authorities vary from area to area, according to local priorities and the requirements of each community; but all are administered in the face of constant interruptions by army attacks. The army counterinsurgency strategy calls for the wholesale elimination of the civilian population from these areas. So while these councils owe their existence to the armed insurrection which put control of the zones into the hands of the people, the context of the war means that hospitals are run without medicines or doctors, food is grown in semi-clandestinity and often destroyed before it can be harvested, supplies are obtained rarely and at great risk. By now, there is hardly a house left standing in many areas, yet the people choose to stay; the future they have fought for is no longer a distant hope, but a concrete experience. Clara gave us some idea of what this means to the people who live in the zones of guerrilla control in El Salvador:

> Because of the experience we have had we cannot go back to the situation as it was before; we cannot go on with the war for ever,

but one day things will be better. Look, we have been fighting for 400 years — the worst is past, only the easier part is left! We have to get through it. That is the reason we are prepared to suffer all of this.

If we go to the city we will not be able to survive there; there we have nothing. And how can we abandon our husbands and children who are fighting for us all? We identify with the guerrillas because they protect us: before, if somebody had a weapon it was to oppress us with, this is the first time that there has been anyone to protect us from the repression. The army has always repressed us. In a village called "El Cedro", the *Batallón Belloso*, which had just come back from being trained in the United States, arrived in the town of 350 people; they stayed four hours and left 131 people dead — unarmed villagers. The most horrible thing was that first they shot the people and then the soldiers cut the bodies to pieces with machetes. This is a psychological measure, since they say that we are now so used to seeing corpses it is more effective to cut up the bodies in pieces to make us more afraid. They think that in this way they are going to make us leave the zone. I was in the town one day after the massacre — I could not stop myself vomiting, and for some nights I couldn't sleep.

Despite the massive financial investment of the United States in the war and the incalculable effect that the conflict has had on the Salvadorean people, the end is not in sight for either side. All that can be predicted with certainty is that the suffering will continue. But the war itself is not measurable solely in terms of military losses and gains: objectively, it is an experience in the collective life of a whole people that affects each one of them. It is a process that cannot just be wiped from memory. In real terms, its impact marks a turning point in the history of El Salvador which defines both the years before and those to follow.

It is at this level that the strength of the forces which oppose the kind of historic solution sought by the US and its Salvadorean allies is most apparent. As a member of the outlawed Revolutionary Democratic Front put it to us in Mexico City:

The problem of the United States is that it fails to understand the development of the internal conflicts of different countries, imagining that they are small and weak, and therefore the problem can be solved by external intervention. It cannot.

The war is a process that cannot just be wiped from memory; its impact marks a turning-point in the history of El Salvador.

The people have learned that they are not too stupid to learn to read and write, nor too lazy to manage their own affairs, as they had always been taught.

6
Free-Fire

What the death squads did on the ground, the Air Force now
does from the air.

María Julia Hernández, *Tutela Legal*,
Archdiocese human rights office.[9]

Colonel Siegfried Ochoa, the outspoken and ambitious former
military commander of Chalatenango and favourite of the US
military establishment (he has since been posted to Washington),
gave a press conference in January 1985 in which he outlined the
army's strategy in the department. As reported by an American
correspondent:

> ...the programme in Chalatenango prohibits civilian movement
> or residence in 12 free-fire zones. Air strikes and artillery
> bombardments are now being carried out indiscriminately in
> these areas, the military leader said.
>
> "In these zones", said Colonel Ochoa, pointing to 12 red areas
> on a provincial map, "there are no civilians. There are only
> concentrations of guerrillas, so we keep these areas under heavy
> fire ..."
>
> Relief officials in San Salvador, however, say that civilians do
> reside in the free-fire zones.[10]

In the conflict areas, anything that moves is a target; there is no
distinction between guerrillas and residents. "There are no
civilians", said Colonel Ochoa; "They're not our civilians" Chief of
Staff Blandón was reported to reply in September 1983 when his
pilots objected to orders to bomb the heavily populated town of
Tenancingo, in which at least 100 residents were killed.[11]
The distinction between a designated free-fire zone and other
areas of conflict between government and rebel forces is also

meaningless. When the bombs rained down on the inhabitants of Tenancingo, for example, the town was not under the control of the guerrillas — but it was a strategic military target in the heavily contested Guazapa region.

Since the bombing of Tenancingo the air war has been intensified dramatically, due to the increase of US military aid to the Salvadorean Air Force. In some areas bombing is almost a daily occurrence, stepped up to saturation point preceding the military operations when the soldiers sweep through the zone. When the army attacks, the people take flight in a mass exodus to seek safety. These are peasant families who already suffer chronic health problems from the lack of basic services and facilities and the shortage of medicines and doctors, exacerbated by seven years of war.

By now, the lands where they live have become no-man's-land.

Mothers run with their children into the mountains, carrying the youngest; other women may be pregnant; there are few adult men, but a great many old people and young children. They grab, if there is time, some bottles of sugared water and a handful of *tortillas* (a dry pancake of ground corn, the staple of the peasants' diet), prepared ready for the operations which always come without warning, and they flee in what they call the *guinda*: a mass withdrawal to the hills.

Charlie Clements, an American volunteer doctor and pacifist who lived with the population of the Guazapa area, a zone mostly controlled by the guerrillas, described the preparations of a village community for flight in his book, *Witness to War*:

The young children of Copapayo — several of whom I'd delivered — were my gravest concern. They were hysterical with fright. They screamed each time the mortar clusters began their descent. They clawed and tore at their mothers, desperate to escape the explosions.

There was no choice but to quiet them.

I crushed my store of tranquilizer tablets and mixed them with orange juice and brown sugar. Then, as each three-whump! salvo was over, I began zigzagging my way from trench to trench.

Sitting still in the trenches, the women were as impassive during the bombardment as stone figures from a Mayan relief. None of the mothers questioned what I was doing: they knew death too well. Each cooed, *'Dulce, dulce'*, (candy, candy) as I dosed their terrorized infants according to my best guess of

individual weight. By dark, there wasn't a conscious child under
three years old in Copapayo.

Then the *guinda* (evacuation) began . . . [12]

It is unclear how the Spanish word for "sour cherry" came to be
used to describe the evacuation of civilians from a military
invasion, but in El Salvador the event has by now become so
commonplace that the noun has come to be used as a verb, and most
of the people who live in or come from the rural areas have had to
guindiar again and again for fear of being caught by the advancing
troops. Past army massacres of communities in the areas of conflict
have taught them that they cannot take the chance of staying in
their homes.

The following account of the evacuation of civilians was
recorded by a Salvadorean priest caught in an attack in San Vicente
province in 1984. He was with the people in the zone to celebrate
Easter, and had taken a tape-recorder to record the service — but
instead he produced an eye-witness account of a flight for life which
lasted almost three weeks:

The others set out last night from the north-west, and we are now
rushing to leave before the army's advance reaches us. This is
how we live here.

We are preparing our own *Via Crucis* [literally, the way of the
cross, a ceremonial re-enactment of Christ's walk to Calvary,
traditionally performed at Easter in the Catholic faith] — our
guinda: to march through the hills carrying what little we can,
children, women and old people; without being able to carry
enough food to eat; climbing over ravines, crags, cliffs, up into the
mountains; stumbling through thorns and bearing a load of
suffering. But that is how things are here . . . .

[Later] The march began at 9.30 this morning. It is a procession
of some 200–300 people. The path is hard and the sun is fierce. It
is a march in search of life, to escape those who want to kill us; it
is the march of a people toward their liberation . . . .

[One day later: Good Friday 20 April 1984] Our *Via Crucis*
continues: last night we stopped to sleep under some trees, at the
edge of a dry cliff which we could use as a trench in case of
bombings or mortars. Now we are no longer 250 people, but at
least 1,500, so many more have joined us. The children walk
barefoot, all the time suffering pain from the thorns. We had
problems crossing the Río Lempa because we had only a single
canoe and because we had been warned that the army was
advancing towards us — the *Atlacatl* and the *Ramón Belloso*

"Our guinda: to march through the hills carrying what little we can, children, women and old people. It is a march in search of life".
Civilian evacuated to a church refugee centre after fleeing an Army operation.

[US-trained elite counterinsurgency battalions], units that have characterised themselves by their crimes against the people.

This morning the march set out at 8.00; we collected our few things together, still wet from the river crossing, and started walking. At 9.30 we could hear in the distance bombs and mortars being dropped on the place where we had spent the night. Now it looks like they are aiming them towards us here. So we are waiting, trying to balance between life and death. Here it is not just at Easter that we live the *Via Crucis*, but every day of the year . . . .

A plane just flew overhead. It is always much more difficult to move when there are planes. We can hear the murmur of a waterfall, the sound of the wind, the noise of the aircraft and the crying of a child; a child who doesn't know anything about war — and yet is suffering here in this war.

Most of us haven't eaten more than a small piece of *tortilla*, cold, because we cannot risk lighting a fire. Some, who have nothing, have to share what food there is with the others, and all must share the hunger.

It is now 1.45 p.m.; right now, as well as the Push-and-Pull [spotter] planes that are flying above us, there is an A-37 bomber, and it has just dropped its first deadly load. We are ready to flee at any moment. We hope that we will be able to get out alive. You can hear [in the background of the tape recording] the explosion of the bombs and the roar of the plane above us. Now it is turning to circle for another run to drop its cargo of death — the people are terrified. We mustn't make any noise, but the children are crying — and who can keep them quiet?

Now it is not the bombs you can hear but the machine-guns of the A-37 sweeping through the zone — the minutes are like hours and the hours like eternities; how we long for night to come so that we can move . . . .

We have walked for an hour, sometimes running because in the distance we can see the army on the hill. We have found more people in flight; now we are more than 2,000. It is shocking to see the parents running with one child in their arms and three or four more following behind, and old people with sticks to help them move. We have arrived at a river with crystal clear water, but there is the noise of helicopters and so we must go on, exhausted, hot, hungry and thirsty . . . .

Now it is 6.30 at night; we are about to set out again, not knowing where we can go. While we were here we were attacked with mortars — 105 mm cannons. There was a great confusion among the people and everyone started running — we fled in panic to seek refuge from the missiles, but we were in the open and there was nothing we could do but wait for the mortars to fall. It was terrible, and I saw a child who had been wounded . . . .

We are still marching, a column passing by the bodies of our fallen companions; we could hardly make them out in the darkness because it is too dangerous to use any lights. Walking at night is very difficult. I don't know how we will be able to survive . . . .

For twenty days the huge column kept moving, pursued by the soldiers, until finally the people were able to go back to their homes — which they found burned down when they got there. Most of the people were lucky enough to survive their ordeal this time, but the priest has since had to abandon his country for exile.

7
Total War

In the conflict zones, there simply aren't any civilians.

The people who move in zones of rebel persistence are identified as guerrillas. Good people — those who are not with the guerrillas — are not there.

Colonel Carlos Aviles, army press spokesman.[13]

"Operation Phoenix" was launched by the army at dawn on 10 January 1986, on the area around the extinct volcano of Guazapa, territory controlled by FMLN forces since the start of the civil war. Like other areas liberated from government control, Guazapa has been the target of artillery barrage, aerial bombardment and infantry sweeps for more than five years, without seriously weakening the rebels' control of the territory. Yet Operation Phoenix was proclaimed by the army as its greatest success of the whole war to date: the reason it was successful is that its actual target was not the guerrillas but the civilian population: it was so successful that at the end of the operation there was hardly a civilian left in Guazapa. The operation was the most concerted attack the army had launched on the rebels' rearguard, involving more than 5,000 troops and lasting two months before residents were cornered and captured near the tiny hamlet of Mirandilla where they had taken their last refuge.

Some of those who survived described what they had been through during those two months:

My name is Mario. I come from the hamlet of El Zapote in Guazapa where I was born.

I want to tell you about Operation Phoenix.

It began with constant bombing from dawn until midday; then came a huge number of soldiers by land.

We had to leave everything just thrown down in our huts, because there wasn't time to do anything, and we fled into the mountain searching for a place to hide. If they find us in our homes they kill us. While I was running I saw the bodies of some people who had been killed by the bombs.

We spent three days without eating anything, without even water to drink since we were hiding among rocks in the mountain. We knew that if we left, the soldiers would kill us. After five days the children began to cry because of the hunger and thirst.

Just there they ambushed a group of more than 40 people, men, women and children, and they captured about 20; four were wounded by machine-gun fire, and three were killed. I only knew the name of one of them, Reyes Nicolás López: he was 48 years old, a day labourer.

We felt desperate because they were pursuing us tirelessly, they didn't give us a chance to sleep or to eat or anything. Everywhere they went they burned the houses they passed, and the corn. If they found clothes that we had buried they burned those too.

There are only civilians there — the fighting is against the civilian population. Wherever they hear the slightest noise, the soldiers shoot; but it's often only people looking for water for the children who are in hiding . . . [14]

The army claimed that there were between 400 and 800 guerrillas in Guazapa at the start of the operation, but the Salvadorean press reported one field commander as saying that they had been unable to find them. What they did find was a civilian population, previously estimated to number about 1,500 people; of these, more than 1,000 were forcibly evacuated from their homes and some 250 were killed.[15]

"The object of this operation is to get rid of the impression in the world that Guazapa belongs to the terrorists", said Colonel Leopoldo Hernández, commander of the First Brigade and of this operation, which also employed three elite US-trained "hunter" battalions. When asked by reporters about civilians living in the area Chief-of-Staff General Adolfo Blandón said, "The civilians who accompany the terrorists are collaborators", implying that they are fair military targets.[16]

We could hear the sounds of distant explosions from San Salvador, as we had on several previous occasions: Guazapa is less than 20 miles due north-east. It was one of the few occasions that the reality of the war outside reached into the heart of the capital, and some of the people we knew were suffering a lot as the dull eruptions punctuated those days, afraid for the lives of relatives they had left behind.

Soon after, in Morazán another operation was launched, although quickly abandoned after heavy army losses, and in Chalatenango "Operation Chavez" got under way in March, uprooting a further 1,200 people. Operations were also carried out in Cabañas, San Miguel, San Vicente and Usulután during the first half of 1986. By September, the army had mobilised more than 20,000 men, almost half its total strength, for a generalised offensive against the population in these areas of the country.[17]

The operations are carried out in areas of intense conflict between the army and FMLN forces — yet most victims are civilians, mainly women, children and old people:

When the army came we saw them destroying the houses, and we were fleeing, as we always do; we spent 22 days in flight. They smashed down the houses and destroyed the orchards and the cornfields. When they captured us they said that they were going to respect our lives — but what is that supposed to mean? If they have destroyed our food, they are not respecting our lives. Because what does a person live on — on rice, corn, and beans; there's nothing left to eat there and we can only die of hunger. So whether we want to or not we have to leave.

We were captured and taken to San Francisco [a farm used as a processing centre by the army] where we were kept 12 days captive. They told us we didn't have the right to be in the places we had come from! Well, are we not Salvadoreans and don't we have the right to live in human dignity in our homes? We were born there and we have our plots of land where we build our houses . . . .

The soldiers said we were pigs, living in the mountain, but we are human beings and we believe in God . . .[18]

Classic revolutionary theory bases the strength of guerrilla forces on the fact that they are hidden amongst and supported by the mass of the people, like fish in the sea; in counterinsurgency doctrine the prescribed remedy is to "drain the sea", and in El Salvador this has been implemented literally. Techniques originally developed in South-East Asia are being applied wholesale in the countryside of this Central American republic.

In an interview with a right-wing magazine in the United States, a

Salvadorean army colonel adapts the metaphor of draining the sea to describe the counterinsurgency strategy in his country:

> Take the population away from the guerrillas, that's the way to win. It's like malaria in this area. You can do two things: you can treat people with malaria for as long as you stay in the area, for the next 3,000 years maybe, or you can drain the swamp and not have to worry about malaria any more . . .[19]

In practice, this means indiscriminate bombing raids, razing of villages, burning of crops and destruction of the means to survive: scorched earth.

For the FMLN guerrillas, operations like Phoenix do not appear to present major difficulties: casualties are not high and their ability to abandon an area, regroup and execute their own operations in their own time, appears to be largely unimpaired. Despite more than 20 major military operations in the last six years and almost daily bombing, the army has been unable to dislodge the guerrillas from the mountain fortress of Guazapa. Operation Phoenix has not prevented guerrilla actions continuing in the area, and even after its "success" the actual extent of government control in Guazapa may be no more than about 40 square kilometres.

The major effect of the escalation of counterinsurgency operations has been to reduce the rebels' ability to protect civilians who live in zones of guerrilla control. A well-trained guerrilla unit can manoeuvre through the lines of a military advance; but civilians, fleeing with children, the old and the sick, are sitting ducks. In fact, the counter-revolutionary war is directed less against FMLN forces themselves than against what the military claims is their base of support: the peasants. The army has declared war on its own people.

The war in El Salvador is part of a strategy formulated in the United States which is being implemented at a regional level throughout Central America, and which draws heavily on the lessons of Vietnam. It has been termed "low-intensity conflict", but military theorists in less guarded moments have described it as "total war at the grassroots level".[20]

A recent analysis of the new tactics concludes:

> U.S. strategists, therefore, would not expect to win by outfighting the enemy in battle. Instead, they would aim to separate the enemy from the civilian population, and neutralise enemy social structures — whether embryonic ones in FMLN zones of control,

or the more institutional kind in revolutionary Nicaragua . . . . This new style of warfare attacks the rebel rearguard, not its main force units, in an effort to destroy the enemy's intelligence, logistical and support systems.[21]

The strategy is long-term and comprehensive, coordinating economic, political, psychological and military tactics whose aim is to establish an overall system of control in the society, which will exclude alternative forms of expression: the body-count this time is not in dead guerrillas but in live civilians.

As a result, the traditional way of life of the peasant farmers and their families in much of the countryside of El Salvador has been shattered. Since the war began, one million people have been forced to seek safety abroad, and more than half as many again have fled or have been forcibly evicted to the cities, to eke out a marginal existence in rapidly growing slums; tens of thousands more have been killed by the army. More than a quarter of the entire population has been made homeless. Those who remain in disputed rural areas live in constant fear of attack, in fear of planes and helicopters flying in over the horizon without warning, of having to run blindly for shelter — perhaps spending many days in a hole in the ground without food or water, or walking in the mountains, hungry, trying to hide.

Advised by US strategists, the army talks of "total war" and "an integral war of attrition"; these jargon terms describe tactics and methods of operation that were employed 15 years ago in Vietnam — with counter-productive results even then. Operation Phoenix is a name that brings back bloody memories: this and other rural pacification operations carried out in conjunction with it in El Salvador are faithful reproductions of Vietnam's "Civil Operations and Rural Development Support" (CORDS) programme of 1967–72: CORDS coordinated the efforts of military, CIA and intelligence agencies, including the notorious *Phoenix* assassination programme.[22] In Vietnam, the distinction between insurgents and ordinary civilians became blurred until it disappeared altogether in practical terms. The *Phoenix* programme alone was credited by the CIA with 20,587 suspects killed (the South Vietnamese government claimed 40,994 "kills") — yet at the end of that programme there was no corresponding decline in US estimates of the number of Viet Cong agents still at large.[23]

A generalised offensive targeted against broad social groups, such as "rural-dwellers", becomes in practice less an operation to eliminate insurgency, more a war of an unrepresentative armed force against a whole people: a tactic doomed to failure as a means of removing pressure for social change. In Vietnam, the advocates of counterinsurgency solutions to the problems of fighting a guerrilla war were unable to prevent the escalation of that conflict, to the point where US bombers turned half the Vietnamese countryside into a blasted desert; in El Salvador the US advisers speak of "low-intensity conflict" — but the war is low-intensity only from the point of view of the United States. For the villagers in the countryside of Guazapa, Morazán and Chalatenango, where hardly a single house is left standing, it has already destroyed their lives.

As the first groups of civilian refugees from Operation Phoenix emerged from a week of interrogation and indoctrination by army intelligence and psychological operations teams, we were able to interview some of them in one of the four refugee centres run by the Catholic Church in San Salvador. The Calle Real camp was opened in the summer of 1985 and has an ominous air of permanence in comparison with the shanty conditions of the other centres — improvised church annexes filled with fold-away beds; Calle Real is custom-built, long wooden barracks divided into sections each sleeping eight to ten people on rough bunks. From a few hundred at the beginning of 1986, the camp's population had mushroomed to more than 1,000 by the end of February. When we were there, 100 tired and frightened peasants from Guazapa had arrived the night before, not knowing where they were being taken. We found children whose hair was falling out in handfuls, malnourished and infested with parasites, old men staring blankly into space, and pregnant women; one woman had given birth in detention. We watched as, even after the trauma of their ordeal, a group of new arrivals began to clear an empty plot of land at the camp — to grow some corn and beans as they have done all their lives in the mountains of Guazapa. These people have become used to having to start over again.

We asked them: what had they done when the planes came? Their replies were cautious at first, but as we crouched in the dusty soil under the shade of a banana tree they seemed to take confidence, and told us how Phoenix had felt from the other side:

Since we have been through bombings before, we watch the planes to see where they are flying and where they are dropping the bombs and machine-gunning. That way we know where to crawl to, more or less. This is how we always protect ourselves during the operations. We flee to where the planes are bombing the least. Sometimes we crawl along the furrows of the fields.

Children whose hair was falling out in handfuls, malnourished and infested with parasites.

We were in flight from the 10th [January] until we were captured on the 25th . . . . When the soldiers were about a mile away we went down to the shacks we have, made from sheets of corrugated iron because there are no houses there, to look for food. We were eight days without anything to eat . . .

We asked them who had destroyed their houses?

They were destroyed by the army — our own government's soldiers. Most of them were destroyed by bombs, and they set fire to those that were left with gasoline . . . during this operation they also burned the cornfields.

The day before we were captured, they found another family about 100 meters below where we were — we could hear their voices and the children crying. I told the others to keep quiet because the soldiers were near, and we stayed there. The following day they came round above us; there were soldiers above and below. They told us we had to come out or they were going to bomb the ravine. We couldn't defend ourselves so we decided to take our chances. On many occasions they kill you, especially the men — that's what we were afraid of.

What did the army say to you? Can you go back to your homes?

We have no rights. We want to return to our homes, but only if we can live like human beings. We have been forced to leave the lands that we work, and we should have the right to return, but the army doesn't allow us — they said, "you'll see what happens to those who go back . . . ."

8
Change and Counter-Change

In El Salvador, counterinsurgency strategy is clearly aimed at non-combatants, targeted by the army as a military objective. "Pacification" and "counter-insurgency" are clean words for what used to be called "counter-terror" — in practice just plain terror. The Green Berets have exported counter-guerrilla warfare all through Latin America, with special investments in El Salvador — a country the size of Wales which receives one quarter of the entire US Latin American aid budget.[24] According to the rebel Radio Venceremos, Operation Phoenix in January 1986 was costing the army $1 million a day.

The Salvadorean army talks about "rescuing" civilians who are evacuated during these operations — while the civilians say they have been captured under fire. Those who have been killed are presented by the army as "guerrillas". In a homily in April 1986 the Archbishop of San Salvador, Monsignor Rivera y Damas, denounced the rape of a young girl by soldiers during Operation Phoenix and the murder of three other minors — during Operation Chavez — who were left by government troops disfigured and with their ears cut off in classic death-squad style.[25]

Earlier, in October 1985, Monsignor Rivera had visited the Guazapa area. The civilian population of the zone begged the Archbishop to denounce the effects that indiscriminate bombing raids and army operations were having on their lives; it was in fact the first time since the beginning of the war that they had had access to any representative of the Church hierarchy. In January 1986 the Archbishop made a pastoral visit to another conflict zone, this time in Chalatenango, where he witnessed a bombing raid at first hand, even, according to the rebel Radio Venceremos, having to take refuge himself. In a sermon broadcast from Chalatenango, he said that hundreds of peasant villages had asked him to speak out for them:

There is a large population of civilians here: it is not true that there are no civilians. My petition is clear: I make myself the voice of all and express to those who should hear — that the bombings should be stopped in areas inhabited by civilians.[26]

On his return he confirmed having seen the attack, contradicting the denial of the Defence Minister, General Vides Casanova, that it had ever taken place. He continued:

I have seen for myself what you who live in these areas want. I have heard your plea not to be moved from these lands where you were born, where you work and suffer, and where you want to continue to live. I have seen your desire for peace, and your desire that military incursions and indiscriminate bombing raids stop, and above all, that international law governing these situations be applied.[27]

The deliberate and systematic policy of depopulation being carried out in the mountains and villages of El Salvador is in violation of international law under the Geneva Conventions of 1949, of which both El Salvador and the United States are signatories. Protocol II of 1977, signed and ratified by the government of El Salvador, specifically relates to the protection of victims of non-international armed conflict. Non-combatants, whether or not they live in close proximity to the guerrillas, whether or not they provide non-military support to the guerrillas and irrespective of their ideology, are considered civilians under the Conventions.

The Duarte government refuses to recognise the applicability of these agreements to the conflict in its country, but the Special Representative of the UN Human Rights Commission has stated, in his report of February 1985, that unarmed civilians in El Salvador, even if they accompany the FMLN or provide the rebels with logistical support, retain their status and are protected by the Geneva Conventions.

Article 13 (2) of Protocol II states:

The civilian population as such, as well as individual civilians, shall not be the object of attack. Acts or threats of violence the primary purpose of which is to spread terror among the population are prohibited.

Under the Conventions, civilians are entitled not to be killed or terrorised, not to be bombed, strafed or mortared, not to be hunted like animals; not to have their homes destroyed (Article 13), their

The deliberate and systematic policy of depopulation being carried out in the mountains and villages of El Salvador is in violation of international law.

crops burned or livestock slaughtered or drinking water poisoned (Article 14).

Article 17 (2) of Protocol II provides that: "Civilians shall not be compelled to leave their own territory for reasons connected with the conflict."

All these are tactics used routinely by the Salvadorean military as part of a deliberate strategy to eliminate whole populations from "enemy" territory, that is, Salvadorean territory; they are war crimes according to the standards of international humanitarian and customary law.[28] The programme has been stepped up dramatically in proportion to the massive inputs of money from the Reagan Administration which the presence of the Christian Democrats in government has allowed. El Salvador receives the fifth greatest allocation of US military aid in the world (1985), and is of course the major Latin American recipient. Spending has been concentrated particularly on building up the air force, in an attempt to win a war in the air that the army has been unable to win on the ground.

The air force has more than doubled its firepower in this period. In 1985 alone additions included:

Six Hughes-500 high speed combat helicopters, some of which carry three M134 7.62 mm machine-guns (called "Muttering Death" in Vietnam) capable of firing 6,000 rounds per minute (rpm) each — that is, 100 bullets every second.
Twelve UH-1M "Iroquois" helicopter gunships which will shoot 4,000 rpm and are equipped with rockets and infra-red night-sighting.
Two AC-47 gunships, known as "Puff the Magic Dragon" in Vietnam, carrying three machine-guns mounted on one side of the plane, each firing 1,650 rpm simultaneously, able to circle the target slowly, capable of putting a bullet in every square inch of a football field. They are also equipped with heat-sensitive night vision equipment (heat-sensing technology cannot distinguish between guerrillas and civilians).
Three A-37 "Dragonfly" jet bombers, each of which carries a load of six 500lb bombs or four 750lb bombs.
Also supplied were a number of UH-1H "Huey" helicopters, the standard Vietnam "Death from Above" machine, bringing the air force's total of these to 46 at that time.[29]

In only the first ten months of 1985 a total of 1,081 air attacks against civilian targets were carried out in eleven of the country's fourteen departments.[30] According to figures from the US Embassy, an average of 129 bombs per month (those under 250lb are not counted) were dropped in 1985, most of these being 750-pounders. These are often fitted with "daisy-cutters", a metal rod about a yard long fixed to the nose of the bomb that causes it to explode above the ground at waist height, sending a spray of shrapnel horizontally to a range of about 225 feet for maximum anti-personnel effect;[31] the majority of civilian casualties from the bombings are caused by shrapnel rather than by direct hits. Incendiary bombs are used to set underbrush and woods on fire, turning night into day and forcing the people to abandon their shelters — making it impossible to hide.

In an interview with a US newspaper Lawrence Bailey, a self-confessed North American mercenary working in El Salvador, gave an insider's view of the war — in which he expressed his admiration for the blunt use of terror tactics by the Salvadorean army.

"In the tiny country of El Salvador, the government has turned its forces not on the communist guerrillas, but on the civilian population who support them," he said.

His argument was arresting. He advocated terrorism as if it were apple pie.

He described massacres of scores of villagers he'd seen as brilliant strategy . . . .

Bailey contends that there is a striking difference between news reports of the El Salvador war and what actually takes place in the field.

"The difference is the target of attack. The army is not killing communist guerrillas, despite what is reported," he said. "It is murdering the civilians who side with them."

"It's a beautiful technique," Bailey said. "By terrorising civilians the army is crushing the rebellion without the need to directly confront the guerrillas," he said.

Bailey contends that the massacres of civilians are not scattered human rights abuses in an otherwise traditional war.

"Attacking civilians is the game plan," he said. From the talks he has had with others in his political camp in El Salvador, and from what he has seen in the field, the strategy is clear: "Kill the sympathisers and you win the war," he said.[33]

These tactics have been the army's response to earlier advances by the guerrillas which at one point looked dangerously close to victory. In June 1983 the army had launched their first comprehensive counterinsurgency effort, the "National Plan", which projected the defeat of the rebels in four phases: firstly, the "cleaning" of key areas (i.e. the physical elimination of the guerrillas), followed by the establishment of Civil Defence units, by "civic–military action" aimed at "reconstruction and development", and finally by resettlement. But the "National Plan" never got to stage two: it was the army rather than the guerrillas who were on the defensive by the end of that year.

In September 1983 the FMLN launched an offensive which culminated in the seizure and destruction of the barracks of the 4th Infantry Brigade in Chalatenango, and the dynamiting of the Cuscatlán bridge, cutting the Pan-American Highway which connects the eastern and western halves of the country. These spectacular actions left the Salvadorean military looking a long way from being able even to contain the rebel threat and forced a rethink in Washington.

The air war was seen as the key to the conflict by US strategists; and the influx of firepower after 1984 did produce tangible, if short-term, results. On the surface things seemed to be going well for the army in 1984 and 1985, as the rebels were forced to avoid the kind of large troop concentrations that had enabled them to take the Chalatenango barracks. At the same time, the drive against the civilian population was projected as a mortal blow to the guerrillas' ability to maintain their supply lines. But to a greater extent FMLN forces have been able to neutralise the advantage of air-power by breaking their forces into small units which carry out a constant stream of minor actions, designed to have maximum impact in terms of material and personnel losses for the armed forces. The idea is that so long as the army has access to practically unlimited supplies of equipment from the United States, the rebels will not be strong enough to overthrow their power; the question is, for how long will supplies be maintained? And so smaller actions aim to wear down the army's morale and to challenge the will of the Reagan Administration (or the US public) to continue funding an expensive long-term war with no end in sight.

At the same time, this dispersal of forces has resulted in the broadening of the theatre of war to engulf the whole country: today, all 14 provinces are war zones. A transport stoppage in January 1987 for the first time demonstrated the guerrillas' ability to control roads in the west as well as the east of the country where they have traditionally been strongest.

Rebel forces have also been able to maintain intact the structures of command they had developed at earlier stages of the war, so that the operational capacity of their forces remains at a sophisticated level. They can concentrate large numbers of troops to carry out an action and then disperse them again within a matter of hours, as

The air war was seen as the key to the conflict by US strategists; and the influx of firepower did produce tangible results.

they proved in October 1985 when guerrilla forces attacked the Armed Forces Training Centre (CEMFA) in La Unión province, holding the base for several hours and causing heavy casualties.[33] Even more spectacularly, in June 1986, the rebels were able to take the country's most important military barracks, the headquarters of the Third Infantry Brigade in San Miguel, in an action reminiscent of the Chalatenango attack — three helicopters were destroyed and the army suffered more than 250 casualties in the assault, according to FMLN figures. In both actions US military advisers were surprised inside the bases.

But political awareness among the people is the most valuable long-term asset of a rebel force in a guerrilla war. It is a priority of the rebel strategy: so long as the conditions which gave rise to the conflict are not resolved, the determination to change those conditions remains among those who suffer because of them, especially since they have learned that they can fight back. The army, under the instruction of its US advisers, is at present implementing a comprehensive strategy that combines "permanent operations", involving massive resources of manpower and fire-power, with psychological tactics designed to undercut the appeal of the revolutionary movement. But these specialised counter-revolutionary techniques attempt to remove the dynamic of change while at the same time maintaining the status quo, simply "cleaned" of its worse excesses. The US strategists recognise that the "counter-revolution must take the revolution out of the hands of the revolutionaries",[34] but without offering structural social change this is no more than wishing that "War is Peace" and "Freedom is Slavery".

The FMLN has turned the dispersal of its forces doubly to its advantage, since this has also enabled it to increase its political work among the people. Each combatant of the three- or four-man FMLN units spread right through the country is encouraged to play the role of educator and organiser, to involve the people in a series of political struggles which aim to challenge the government's record and to expose the role it has chosen to play within the counterinsurgency project. This process in a way extends through-out the country the experience of social reorganisation and grassroots democracy that has been carried out inside the zones of guerrilla control during seven years of conflict. Far from limiting the revolutionary war, the government's strategy has made it all-embracing.

PART THREE

Government Against the People

9
Odyssey

The people of the conflict zones have changed their lives, but at enormous cost — a price levied by the army in lives and in suffering. The country has been physically divided by the war. In real terms, this division can mean being free to work a piece of land that doesn't belong to someone else, where you can grow enough food to eat, perhaps learn to read and write, organise your own way of life and decide what that way of life will be. Yet it can also mean living in constant fear of being attacked without warning; living in a house, or in the bombed shell of what once was a house. Or it might mean living in a shack made of discarded boxes and plastic sheeting, along the railway lines or beside the sewers, wherever you can find a space in the city slums. For those who have to flee the zones, or are forcibly evacuated by the army, life in the cities means a life without a future, a life of dirt and disease, unemployment and poverty; it means living in fear of the security forces, not travelling so as not to get stopped at the road-blocks, not saying anything that might be interpreted against you — and above all, not trying to confront the system that has consigned you, your children and your children's children to such a future.

In 1986, prior to the October earthquake, the drive against civilians was intensified by the army's constant and coordinated operations against the rebels' rearguard areas of Guazapa, Morazán and Chalatenango, and in the provinces of San Vicente and Usulután. In an attempt to defuse international criticism of its policy, and, at the same time, to launch a propaganda campaign designed to win over its own population, the army claimed to be making a new effort to reduce civilian deaths; but it has been faced with the daunting task of persuading those it has bombed and attacked that this has been done for their own good.

In March 1986, for example, a group of 20 men, 24 women and 42 children took refuge in the church of Dulce Nombre de María, a small town in Chalatenango province, fleeing the army's advance during Operation Chavez. One of the refugees later described how, as they were worshipping, the church was surrounded by the soldiers in pursuit:

> We thought that they would not violate the house of God. Yet they came in with their weapons and machine-guns ... one of the soldiers said to us, "The only thing you people understand is a bullet."
>
> We told them that we had the permission of the priests to be there, but they said that they, not the priests, gave the orders. We said that we didn't want to leave, but they said that if we didn't agree they would take us out by force.
>
> They pushed the men into one truck and the women and children into another; many were crying, we were all very scared.
>
> They took us to the military barracks at Chalatenango ... they gave us a talk about what life is like for the people who live in the socialist countries, the countries of Russia where they said the people are poor because they are lazy. And they spoke about Comandante Castro of Cuba, how he had killed the priests; but I thought about how here in El Salvador the government had killed many priests, nuns too, and even our Archbishop, Monsignor Romero ....
>
> Later the Red Cross came and the Colonel said we could go where we wanted. We all said we wanted to go back to our homes in San José las Flores ... but when the Colonel saw that we wanted to return he said we were just subversives and we only wanted to go back to make trouble. He gave us just two alternatives: either we go with the Red Cross to one of the church refugee centres or we stay there in the barracks to be interrogated.[1]

Those who escape the advancing troops undertake their flight out of desperation and in conditions of extreme danger and hardship. Peasants from the northernmost provinces try to seek safety across the national border in Honduras. In an unpublished account, a journalist who was present in the camp in November 1985 described the arrival of a large group of refugees to Colomoncagua, a refugee camp in southern Honduras:

> On Sunday night, November 3, a group 134 men, women and children wandered into the camp, suffering from hunger, exhaustion and exposure. Another group of nine arrived on Wednesday, the 6th.
>
> In many cases the refugees had fled their former homes when

they were bombed in previous years (a number were originally from Perquín [in northern Morazán province]) and had lived a nomadic existence, finding abandoned houses in other settlements and staying until they too were bombed. Some of the refugees had lost family members in two or three stages this way.

Few of the men were under 40. Areas of their skin, especially their feet, were covered with bleeding sores. Several of the women were pregnant.

Several of them independently said that, following the bombing or attack on their homes they fled to the hills where they began to gather, first a dozen, then several dozen, until there was a large number. Some of them were aware that Honduras lay to the north. As they headed north, they continued to pick up more numbers, mostly one by one. An unknown number of the group, mostly women and children, died of disease or exhaustion along the way.

They all said that they knew of no guerrilla camps near [i.e. within bombing range of] their settlements. When asked what the bombing targets seemed to be, they consistently answered "*el mero pueblo*" ("the town itself"). They said the bombings were accompanied by ground assaults, perhaps some parachute troops, razing of houses, capture and killing of civilians, and crop-burning.

One of the refugees, a 23-year-old woman, gave this testimony of her odyssey:

For three years I have been wandering, ever since the first bombardment that destroyed my house. Lately I was living for a month in La Tijera. I lived with a family, but they all died in the house. There was the old man, Felipe García, the grandfather, and Wilfredo Romero, 6 months old.

Around the house were more people who died. When we saw the planes, we left. Only the ones in the house died. We went to hide in the mountain.

The Army came in the next day. There were 22 planes and helicopters. We hid in the mountain and they were looking for us. They captured some men and took them away. There was a 60-year-old man named Juan Rosa from Los Patios, Sabanetas.

They beat him a lot. I saw it, I was hiding on the hilltop. It was the Arce battalion, the Lenca, the Cuscatlán and Morazán battalions. I know because they said they were from there, they were chanting it, and they wrote the names on the wall, they painted them on the rocks, walls, on everything, saying that we were going to die.

Some women died on the road. We walked through the mountains, we lost all our clothes. We knew that Honduras was here, that was all. I'm pregnant, not long to go. When we didn't hear shots we knew we could keep walking. We joined with another group. Everyone was in the mountains searching for a path.

Even this journey may not bring the people to safety; the Colomoncagua camp has been surrounded by a cordon of Honduran troops since May 1985 in an attempt to deter new arrivals. The Honduran government wants to repatriate all the refugees to El Salvador, despite the fact that the conditions that caused the people to flee have not improved. In August 1985 the Honduran military attacked the camp: an eye-witness described how the soldiers forced their way in and started shooting wildly in all directions. She said they seemed to be drugged. They grabbed some of the refugees and tortured one man in front of everyone in the camp, including the UNHCR's (United Nations High Commissioner for Refugees) official. A two-month-old baby was killed, kicked to death; the soldiers blew off the head of a 23-year-old man; and two young girls were raped in the schoolroom.[2]

Refugees are the most tangible product of the counterinsurgency war. Those unable to escape abroad have remained within the national borders, and it is these internal refugees who are referred to as the "displaced". They are the shattered survivors of the poorest sectors of Salvadorean society; physically displaced, they are also socially and psychologically dislocated, a generation growing up in the shadow of the war. The families themselves show the characteristics of casualties of conflict, as a detailed investigation undertaken by the Jesuit University (UCA) makes clear: more than half the family members are youths and children, although fewer than average young children have survived; old people too were recorded to be fewer than the national average. In particular, the figures show a significant imbalance in the adult male population, leaving many women to shoulder the whole burden of bringing up their families.[3] The same study shows that most of those who have fled have done so "because of the fear of repression and of the army — in very few cases out of fear of the guerrillas".[4]

Moreover, almost all (80–90%) of the families were previously peasant farmers dependent on working the land to make a living; the people are overwhelmingly illiterate, sharing an almost total

*Refugees are the most tangible product of the counterinsurgency war.
In a UNHCR camp in southern Honduras.*

lack of formal education. This makes it impossible for them to find employment in the few factories of the cities.[5]

Some end up in government-run camps and another small proportion are able to find a place in various church refugee centres, most notably those of the Catholic Archdiocese, which opened the first centre for the displaced in March 1980 under the direction of Monsignor Romero. But by far the majority (some 95%) of these people drift to burgeoning slums around the capital and other cities. The greatest concentration is in San Salvador, where the people continue to squeeze themselves into the overcrowded squatter-camps that surround the city. Over 200,000 of these people were uprooted again by the earthquake that struck the capital in October 1986. In all cases, the displaced make up a marginalised population living in conditions of severe deprivation and physical, social and economic dependence and insecurity. They are also a target for harassment by the security forces, who regard the displaced as suspicious simply because they come from areas where the FMLN–FDR are active.

We asked a priest who lives with the displaced in his parish — a mess of narrow lanes and home-made dwellings held together with sticks and stones — what the situation was like for the people he was trying to help:

I think that the problem of the displaced is the most serious product of the war which is going on in this country. It is a problem for which there is no sign of a solution or of a move towards a solution; on the contrary, it is getting worse all the time. This is going to have drastic consequences: of uprooting the people, of their difficulties in adapting, of work — because there isn't any — of housing, health and so on.

Those who come here do so because they have relatives or friends who can take them in for a while, or help them to find a place to put up a shack. But you can see, there are no places. Every space is completely crammed. There are gullies where the people put their shacks and when the level of the river rises they are all flooded, yet all these gullies and ravines are full; or they find a tiny space along the sides of the railway line, where the land belongs to the municipal authorities.

Health is one of the biggest problems we have since the people don't have any money to go to the few clinics there are, and so they live in a terrible misery, suffering chronic sickness: illnesses caused by malnutrition, parasites, anaemia, lack of hygiene and simply from the lack of a normal lifestyle.

In the long term, there are even more serious problems. For example, among the young a whole generation is growing up having lost their traditional way of life; living in this situation of overcrowding, poverty and misery, this generation will find it very difficult to adapt to the life of the city — or rather to the life of these shanty-towns. And having lost their traditional values, these young people are not going to want to return to their places of origin, because they no longer know how to live there. The problems are not only serious, but also numerous and complex. In the short term, we have no solutions; we can only attend to the most basic immediate needs of the people.

The church distributes some food and we try to help the people to develop a sense of community, so that they don't become only accustomed to taking hand-outs — which creates passivity and dependence: the people become hopeless, isolated and lose their sense of living and working together. All our efforts are designed to encourage the people to collaborate and to share, so that those who receive food must also help others, and take the responsibility of distributing it themselves. But this is very difficult to achieve.

Some displaced families themselves described to us the crisis they are going through:

In the rural areas we kept animals and cultivated crops, and so managed to support our families. We were also able to have somewhere to live, but here in the city things are very different. There are many of us who have spent two or three years here without being able to find work, and because of this our situation has become desperate. We have no homes, no food or medicine; we don't have any of even the most basic things in the shacks we are living in.

If we cannot work, it is not because we don't have the strength, but because we don't have the freedom.

A man of about 30 explained:

The work I can get here in San Salvador is to shine shoes; my wife makes baskets and my children sell newspapers. We can't find any other work because the only thing we know is how to work in the fields. And what we earn is not enough to pay any rent. Sometimes I don't find anyone who wants their shoes cleaned and that day my children don't eat; they cry for food, and then we all cry, even my wife.

Women support their families earning 2 colones (about 30 pence) for an average day's work.

Refugees weave shredded cactus to make baskets and hammocks.

The people survive as best they can, and by whatever means — survival is a full-time job. This leaves them unprotected against manipulation either by local speculators or by the government itself. Handicrafts, such as basket-making or hammock-weaving, are one of the few means of survival for many of the displaced; but they find themselves at the mercy of middlemen who sell them the raw materials and then buy back the finished product and fix the prices at both ends. Women we spoke to who had to support families on their own were earning two *colones* (about 30p) for an average day's work in a camp in San Francisco Gotera, Morazán province.

In general, people who have been evicted from their homes under fire by the army are suspicious of government aid programmes. They are unwilling to give their name, place of origin, present residence, and details of family and dependants as required in order to register for assistance with the government agency, the National Commission to Assist the Displaced (CONADES); especially since the monthly list of registrants is passed to the local army commander. Those who are registered with the government can supplement meagre food aid by finding occasional work (for two weeks only, a maximum of three times a year) on labour projects funded by the US Agency for International Development (AID): workers on these projects earn six *colones* (about 75p or just over $1), less than half the legal urban minimum wage, for tasks such as road building. In one such project, we watched women fetching water and sand, and children pushing wheelbarrows while the men, many of them old, broke piles of rocks with sledge-hammers. A professor we spoke to at the Jesuit University described these projects as "hard work under the burning sun for a hunger wage, which the people have to accept because they have no alternative." CONADES itself is critical of such programmes, alleging that "people are forced to dig a hole and then fill it in." These humanitarian aid programmes administered by the government agencies, or by AID and private agencies contracted to implement AID projects, are also criticised by independent groups who work with the displaced as being dominated by political, counter-insurgency objectives. They have been incorporated into the strategy of the "total war" that overshadows El Salvador.

10
Welfare as Warfare

The displaced population of the country poses an enormous problem for the government, whose own policies have led to such a concentration of people becoming first marginalised and now physically located in the centre of national life — there may be as many as 400,000 in San Salvador alone. This is a constant reminder to their own people and to the international community of the continuing conflict and its cost in human terms. The government cannot simply ignore the displaced, but at the same time it cannot attend seriously to the problem from a developmental point of view because it regards the people as, at best, potential "subversives". Instead, the displaced become once more an "objective" of the counter-insurgency project.

The "total war" against the people of El Salvador does not end when they are forced to abandon their homes. An important evaluation of the government's current "low-intensity" war strategy makes the key observation that, "Low-intensity conflict is extreme: it is a science of warfare whose goal of controlling the qualitative aspects of human life merits the term 'totalitarian'."[6]

In a television broadcast on 11 April 1986, Army Chief-of-Staff General Blandón stated that the displaced were "an integral part of military plans", adding "we want to know their names, where they are going to live, what they plan to do for a living, in order to have control over the population."[7]

At the beginning of 1986, US advisers designed a new "psy-ops" division within the Salvadorean military structure. The Department of Civic–Military and Psychological Operations (S5) was financed out of a $22 million US "counter-terrorist" aid package and intended to combine military operations with civic action programmes, including food-aid, medical care and literacy training.[8] This sophistication of the army's tactics is part of the efforts by the United States to reduce the civil war to a "manageable" level of

The displaced become, once more, an 'objective' of the counter-insurgency project.
Refugees on an AID road-building programme in Morazán province.

violence: a level at which the war itself no longer dominates national life. The aim is to isolate guerrilla activity to the marginal northernmost provinces, while at the same time concentrating psychological warfare tactics in a new civic–military drive, known in jargon terms as "nation-building". But this kind of programme must be judged in the context of the most concentrated bombardment of a civilian population in the history of Latin America.

The current strategy is not different in any significant respect from the kind of psychological operations used in the Vietnam conflict, nor radically different from tactics employed, without success, in El Salvador earlier in the war. The chief distinction is that in the present phase of the war the "nation-building" strategy is to be pursued in a more coherent and more effective way, coordinating "all the weapons of total war including political, economic and psychological warfare, with the military aspect being a distant fourth in many cases."[9]

The concept of "nation-building" offers a rhetoric of reform as cement for a combination of sophisticated political and military counterinsurgency elements. It is based on the recognition that in order to defeat the revolutionary forces it is necessary to create an "alternative" political model around which the population can be convinced to support the government project. This implicitly acknowledges that the revolutionary impetus does command the support of the people and that the government project does not. It recognises, as the Reagan rhetoric refuses to do, that insurgency is not primarily a military but a social problem, and that armed guerrillas, supported by a population who have always lived in dehumanising poverty, cannot be defeated by purely military means.

The Duarte government was originally intended to serve as the cornerstone of this new nation, the "alternative" to the old oligarchy around which sufficient popular support would be mobilised. But for the reasons analysed in Part 1, Duarte failed to implement significant reforms and so failed to achieve a shift in the real focus of power in El Salvador. This lost him his popular support and at the same time left the war at an even more intractable stage. By the end of 1985 his Social Pact was a dead letter. His conduct of the war and of the economy had alienated almost the whole of the coalition of forces which had secured his election. Duarte's failure to build a secure social base for the government's project is specifically due to the fact that the concept of "nation-building" as applied in El Salvador has nothing to do with a genuine attempt to redress injustice and extend participation in the democratic life of the society; what it is is an attempt to manipulate enough of the people through social control and psychological operations to maintain in power a stable government, which, in turn, will safeguard US strategic interests in the region and protect those of its Salvadorean allies.

In practice, the main achievement of the Duarte Administration has been to secure increased levels of military and economic aid from the US Congress for its war effort. This is to some extent ironic, since the United States now seems less committed to supporting Duarte politically against his right-wing opposition and is using aid as a way to strengthen some of his enemies. Funds from the US Agency for International Development (AID) have increasingly been channelled through private Salvadorean and US agencies rather than the government; at the same time, the US has provided extensive backing to organisations representing a "modernising" sector of the traditional elite. Over the past several years AID has spent substantial amounts of money on support for the Salvadorean Foundation for Economic Development (FUSADES) (estimates are as high as $50 million); FUSADES is responsible for the promotion and implementation of Caribbean Basin Initiative policies in El Salvador and is closely linked to a new right-wing political party, *Patria Libre*, which is said to have the blessing of the US Embassy.

The struggle for loyalties is a complex campaign that combines a wide range of elements, of which Duarte is only one part. Aid is a key weapon in the unconventional war: it is a civilian front which allows the Salvadorean government and its US sponsor to paint warfare as charity. A vital component of military psychological operations, humanitarian aid enables the government to control a population which is excluded from the economic life of the society, and dependent on handouts of food for their family's survival: those handouts can be made conditional on participation in government projects, such as civil defence or resettlement in "model" village structures.

In El Salvador, the distribution of aid in areas of conflict (which cover a large proportion of the national territory) has been placed directly in the hands of the army; so that peasants who have lived their whole lives in mortal fear of the soldiers are faced with "military–civic action" projects, in which the army appears in their village for a one-day distribution of food and medicines — amid the fanfare of a brass-band and non-stop loudspeaker broadcasts of anti-communist propaganda. We attended one of these events, and watching as the brightly coloured pills were handed out to children suffering from malnutrition it was hard to see how this would undo the fear and mistrust of the army which has been built up over the past 50 years of military domination. Colonel Ochoa, who had declared large parts of the province of Chalatenango under his command a free-fire zone, and who bombed communities in violation of the 1985 Christmas truce, told us that:

> We have psychological operations so that the people can have confidence in us, and so that the terrorists will not be afraid to give themselves up because now there is no need to carry a gun, now there is democracy.

Psychological operations are no substitute for development; the children in the line at the medical post were given bags of pills of different types to treat sicknesses which are due to endemic poverty, and instructions for dosage were written on labels for people who, like 85% of the rural population of El Salvador, are illiterate.

A professor at the Jesuit University, who works with the displaced, pointed out to us the inconsistency of these tactics:

> Often, the civic–military action programmes are planned in conjunction with military operations — that is, they know that they are going to force the people to flee and afterwards they go and give them some food and medical attention. This is obviously the strategy of a counter-insurgency operation to win the sympathy of the people, but I don't believe that they can so easily convince the person who has just been evicted from his home that the army has changed.

"Beans-and-bullets" strategies of this type require that the aid offered by the government and the army should be the only help available to the people, the better to convince them. Independent agencies and relief officials, particularly those working with the displaced, are subject to obstruction and harassment in order to restrict access to alternatives; while government bodies in charge of the distribution of aid, such as CONADES and the National Commission for the Restoration of Areas (CONARA), which was modelled on the Vietnam CORDS programme, are subject to military control. In Vietnam, the CORDS structure placed under military control all US agencies dealing with pacification and civilian field operations, including AID. In El Salvador the civil authorities must report to army commanders at the local and departmental level, and both CONADES and CONARA receive the major part of their funding from the United States through AID.[10]

In this way, government initiatives are planned in a context that

Psychological operations are no substitute for development.
'Civic–military action' project in Chalatenango province.

deliberately ignores the real needs of the people they purport to help. In 1984, after the failure in 1983 of the "National Plan", the army's first major pacification effort, the government proposed a new initiative known officially as "Project One Thousand" (referring to the 1,000 new communities it aimed to create). The project proposed to resettle half a million people in specially built communities in areas controlled by the government; it was drawn up in consultation with USAID and two of its officials were AID staff — both of whom had worked on the "model village" programme in neighbouring Guatemala (one had served in the CORDS "strategic hamlet" programme in Vietnam). In Guatemala, a brutal "scorched communists" programme of the early 1980s destroyed some 440 Indian villages and left one million displaced people, who were then "resettled" into purpose-built villages where they remain today: each is overlooked by a military base which controls all movements, and one million adult males are obliged to serve in paramilitary "civil" patrols. Coincidentally, the slogan for Project One Thousand in El Salvador was *"Techo-Tortilla-Trabajo"* ("Houses-Food-Work"), the same slogan under which the rural population of Guatemala had earlier been militarised. But the project failed to raise sufficient international funding to get off the drawing-board because of misgivings about its true objectives.

At any rate, it was superseded in July 1986 by another new government initiative. Significantly, it was General Blandón who launched this comprehensive programme to resettle areas devastated by the war, known as "United to Reconstruct", stating at a press conference: "In this war it is not a question of conquering territory, but of conquering the mind and will of the people."[12] The programme appears to repeat the objectives of the abortive National Plan, except that in keeping with the tenets of "nation-building" it intends to combine — under army control — the work of government departments and the private sector, such as business, church and labour organisations, to implement its three phases: the military conquest of all the conflict zones; consolidation of control by establishing civil defence units; and reconstruction. Blandón said that $18 million for the programme would be provided directly by the United States, and this was confirmed by the US Embassy.[13]

Whether or not the programme will in fact be able to win civilian support, and whether or not the army will be able to secure military control of the conflict zones, this militarisation of aid resources must raise questions about their humanitarian content. In the proposals to repopulate war zones such as Guazapa, those who were evacuated during the operations that preceded the new programme are not to be permitted to return; potential residents are government sympathisers who must be registered with CONADES, and the resettlement will be conducted through CONARA.

Development projects are, in this context, a mechanism for winning the hearts and minds of a literally captive audience, and for this reason many independent humanitarian organisations in El Salvador refuse to accept AID funding. And as "aid" has become a weapon to win hearts and minds in the war, the government's dirty war has been used to monopolise development resources, including aid, in support of its own counterinsurgency programme. In this context, both the displaced themselves, and workers from non-governmental humanitarian agencies, face persecution in their efforts to rebuild shattered lives. A priest threatened with expulsion from the country explained to us:

> The government has tried to incorporate the humanitarian agencies into a global plan which seeks to employ all the humanitarian resources that come into the country. Without doubt the independent agencies have opposed this, and so they have created their own organisation and distribution in order to avoid attempts to control their work. Because of this, workers from institutions such as the Catholic Archdiocese or other churches have been unjustly detained, and worse, solely for following a line of work that is not part of the government's programme.

The displaced have to face abuses that are already too familiar to them: detentions at road-blocks, arrests by heavily armed men who come in the night, torture in the prisons and unexplained "disappearances". Many of these people have been evicted from areas where they had created and administered sophisticated forms of communal organisation, and experienced a high level of self-determination; the loyalty of all is suspect. Camps, refugee centres and non-governmental resettlement projects are special targets of surveillance and harassment by the security forces. Usually, the people's identity papers have been lost or destroyed with the rest of their belongings, so they have either no documents or else special "safe-passes" issued by the army which make them easily distinguishable at frequent check-points.

Eugenia, a 26-year-old displaced woman from the Domus María refugee camp in San Salvador, describes what happened to her after she was taken off a bus as she was travelling to visit relatives:

The displaced have to face abuses that are already too familiar to them.

When I gave them my ID card they said that I was suspicious, and they took me to the barracks ... my hands and feet were tied, and I was stripped naked ... three men wearing hoods started to ask me questions . . . they beat me, and they gave me some pills which made me feel dizzy ... they asked me which refugees went to see the guerrillas, how many guerrillas came to Domus María, and who were the wounded guerrillas there. I told them that most of us are women and children and there are no guerrillas there. They threatened that they were going to take away my child, that they would go to the camp and get her. They asked who were the people from the Archdiocese who came to teach us, who were the priests who gave us mass, they wanted me to describe them and to tell them the names of those who brought us food, who gave us medicines, where did they come from ... they asked me which nuns came there to collaborate with the guerrillas, and they said that it would be best to burn the place down and be done with it.[14]

Attempts by the displaced to organise in order to improve their day-to-day conditions are regarded as especially dangerous by the authorities. The priest we met from the capital's slum told us of one such case of "subversion" in his parish:

We wanted to establish a project for the community, to organise the cleaning of the lanes and to put in some more water taps, because there is no running water and only three taps that everyone has to use to collect water; but what happened? — they came and took away the leader of the group, who was detained for 15 days, tortured and then released.

They didn't have any charges against him, it was just to frighten the others — and they were frightened, since the repression here has been enormous.

We were working, and the people were participating well, but now they don't want to come to the meetings because they are afraid. After they released the leader, the police came around a few times to threaten the others, so that the people can't help themselves and improve their lives. This is a problem we have all the time.

Another priest, who works with the displaced in San Salvador, told us that even in the church centres the safety of the refugees from their own government cannot be guaranteed; he described the kind of harassment they receive regularly at the hands of the security forces:

You must realise that these people have suffered so greatly that the presence of an army uniform makes them very nervous — they regard all who wear the uniform as bringers of death. I remember one day when the army came into one of the camps, a tiny and overcrowded place packed with people — it seems like an anthill with so many children running all over the place; but when the soldiers came in, the place suddenly seemed to be deserted. Everyone was hiding in corners and every mother grabbed her children while the soldiers walked around. It was as though there was nobody there. These tactics are used to frighten the people; because sometimes the soldiers see somebody and just take them away. They do this so that the people will not seek protection. They have also arrested those who work there, such as medical personnel.

In the course of their jobs, international humanitarian workers have become familiar with these scare tactics, and have themselves been detained and intimidated. In March 1986, four medical aid workers from the Paris-based organisation Médecins du Monde, an independent agency working legally in El Salvador, were stopped at a road-block as they were driving to a clinic in the eastern city of San Miguel. They were detained, and then taken back to San Salvador to the High Command HQ of the army. They were refused permission to make a telephone call to their embassies or to the coordinator of their mission. From there they were taken to the headquarters of the Treasury Police where again they were denied permission to contact their embassies. For two days they were detained incommunicado, and interrogated about their organisation, their political and trade union affiliation, contacts they had with guerrillas, and especially about the Salvadoreans employed by the organisation — whose names and addresses they had to give. When they were finally released they were told to leave the country.

This is not an isolated phenomenon. In September 1985, members of the AMI (Assistance Médicale Internationale) team were captured in Chalatenango, and in December, workers from Médecins Sans Frontières were also detained by security forces.

Yet workers from international organisations enjoy a greater degree of physical security than do those of domestic agencies, who risk their own lives in their efforts to help others. In May 1986, non-governmental human rights groups in San Salvador were attacked in a series of raids which marked a coordinated attempt to discredit independent agencies and to prevent their continuing criticism of government policy. On 6 May Laura Pinto, international

Workers from domestic agencies risk their own lives in their efforts to help others.

May 1987 — CO-MADRES offices are bombed by unknown assailants.

representative of the Committee of Mothers of Political Prisoners, the Disappeared and Assassinated of El Salvador (CO-MADRES), was seized 100 yards from the CO-MADRES office by three heavily armed men in civilian clothes, driving a car without licence plates. Two days later she was dumped unconscious in a park in the capital; she had been tortured and interrogated in the headquarters of the Treasury Police about the activities of the Mothers Committee — she was stripped, beaten, and raped; she also suffered a deep knife wound to the abdomen for which she had to have surgery.

Just three weeks later, Laura Pinto was again abducted by members of the Treasury Police. After 14 days in detention, during which she was beaten repeatedly and deprived of sleep and food, she was made to sign a confession that she was not allowed to read and then transferred to Ilopango women's prison. She has not been charged with any crime. In an interview from prison taken by a British human rights worker, Laura Pinto described the circumstances of this second arrest on 28 May:

> That afternoon, I was going with a friend to get some medicine for a woman in prison. We weren't far from our office. We'd been followed by a grey van with darkened windows. It stopped and four men jumped out, dressed in plain clothes.
>
> Two of them grabbed me by the arms. I struggled, but a fifth man came out and they shoved me into the van at gunpoint. They asked me my name, and when I told them, one of them called in on a radio: "We've got her"; I heard the reply: "Bring her in".[15]

Laura Pinto was eventually released in September 1986 owing to international pressure, but over 1,000 political prisoners remain in Salvadorean jails.

During the three weeks that separated these two ordeals, nine other members of various Salvadorean human rights organisations were also detained. On 19 May one of them, Michele Salinas, an executive member of the non-governmental Human Rights Commission of El Salvador (CDHES), was taken from her home at 4 a.m. by heavily armed men in civilian clothes, who subsequently turned out to have been from the Treasury Police. After more than ten days in detention Salinas was presented at a television press conference in which she denounced most of the independent domestic humanitarian agencies in El Salvador as being front organisations for the FDR–FMLN rebels. Among the agencies accused were CDHES, CO-MADRES, the Catholic Archdiocese, the Catholic Social Secretariat and Tutela Legal, its human rights office, the Catholic Christian Communities, the Lutheran and Episcopal Churches, the US National Council of Churches, the Christian Committee for the Displaced (CRIPDES), and the Archbishop of San Salvador himself, Monsignor Rivera y Damas.[16]

While Salinas was speaking on television, many of the workers she named were already in the custody of the Treasury Police. During June the detentions and harassment continued. In response, a joint communiqué issued by the Lutheran, Baptist, Episcopal and Catholic Churches rejected the accusations against them and insisted on their right and duty to continue to work with those most seriously affected by the war, in particular the displaced. They catalogued their work: financial help for food production; aid to war-orphan centres; work projects for widows; supply of building materials; community health projects; distribution of food and clothing; and support to the refugee centres. They also stated that it was a priority to end the war and repeated their support for dialogue as the only just solution to the conflict. The answer came back at the end of the month: an anonymous telephone call threatening death for 16 members of various religious organisations. They were given eight days to leave the country.[17]

The reasoning behind these attacks is that work outside the government's structure is seen as opposing government objectives: he who is not my friend is my enemy.

For example, after the catastrophic earthquake which struck the capital on 10 October 1986, the Duarte government set up a committee of business leaders to coordinate the stockpiling of relief supplies and aid from abroad. But it was the military, in keeping with the theories of "low-intensity conflict" behind their "United to Reconstruct" pacification plan, who took on a growing relief role in the actual distribution of supplies. Within El Salvador, many organisations wanted to maintain their independence from this kind of government initiative. In this context, aid which was sent directly from abroad through non-governmental channels — as a response to the worst natural disaster in the country's history — became a political issue and was dealt with in the manner of political issues in El Salvador. Planes loaded with supplies for the Catholic Archdiocese were refused permission to land, as were supplies from Eastern bloc countries which were sent by international labour union federations. One union leader, while helping to dig people out of earthquake rubble, was shot by soldiers who claimed he was looting. And army patrols visited some of the poor neighbourhoods worst affected by the earthquake, asking for the names of those in charge of coordinating the distribution of aid from non-governmental sources; the next day, according to eye-witnesses, on at least two occasions church workers were abducted by the plain-clothes armed men driving vehicles with one-way polarised windows that are the trade-mark of the Salvadorean security force, and death-squad, operations.

11
Orders to Kill

We had heard the testimonies of so many people in El Salvador describing how they, or their friends or family, had been taken away by "heavily armed men dressed in civilian clothes" that I should not have been as shaken as I was when one day in November 1985 I was, myself, faced with four fat thugs, dressed in jeans and carrying lightweight automatic machine-guns. I was handcuffed and blindfolded and bundled into the back of a Cherokee Chief jeep — by dropping my head I could just make out the polarised windscreen that hides its occupants and their actions from outside view.

I had been arrested while trying to photograph, from too safe a distance to succeed, the bombing of the area around the Guazapa volcano which we had been able to hear for the past few days in the capital. Although my credentials were in order when I produced them to show the army patrol I had run into, I was nonetheless detained and flown by helicopter to the military airport, where the sinister reception committee was already waiting.

From there I was taken on a 15-minute drive to an unknown destination and led into a cell, where I was to be held incommunicado for the next three days and two nights. About two metres by three, it was one of a block of perhaps ten or twelve cells built in a square which shared the illumination of a single fluorescent tube through the steel-mesh ceiling. I protested vigorously and demanded to be allowed to contact my Embassy, and my partner, but I was told that there were no telephones there, and I fared no better with my demand to know where "there" was. I was frankly scared, which I told myself was what they wanted; but I didn't get much reassurance from that.

Yet I knew that, as a foreigner and an accredited journalist, I was far luckier than the people whose testimonies I had taken in the union offices and church refuges and *barrios* of San Salvador.

I later discovered that I was in the headquarters of the National

Guard and that the four thugs were National Guard officers. On numerous occasions over the next 48 hours I was asked familiar-sounding questions: Who were my contacts with the guerrillas? Who was I going to meet in Guazapa? Who had I spoken to since I had arrived in El Salvador? I had to account for my movements day by day for the time I had spent in the country. The films I had taken were removed from my camera and processed. At one point I was interrogated by a man wearing a green hood — all I could see were his eyes set into two dark cut-out holes.

But as I knew, I was in a very privileged position; when I didn't return to my hotel my partner had alerted the foreign press who exerted the necessary pressure to get me released relatively quickly. Nevertheless, I felt that the experience had given me an insider's view of the counter-insurgency state, one I wouldn't care to repeat.

A tight control of the foreign press is a priority in the government's current intelligence-gathering operations; several other journalists have subsequently been detained in similar circumstances. In May 1986, three journalists were "captured" during a military operation in Chalatenango and flown to the local barracks by helicopter and questioned for eleven hours. Their taped cassettes of interviews and their camera films were confiscated and their notes photocopied, tactics which in practice destroy the neutrality of the working press by exposing journalists' sources.[18] On 3 November 1986, religious workers from the Catholic Church reported that the army had surrounded the hamlet of San José las Flores in Chalatenango, bringing with them a cassette tape which contained an interview recorded by a group of foreign journalists; the journalists had been detained after visiting the village in September and the tape confiscated. The Colonel then sent out the teachers from the school and played the tape to the children, asking them to identify who was speaking — a 31-year-old man whose voice had been identified in this way was one of several people then taken away for interrogation.

President Duarte has made dramatic claims to be the guardian of human rights in El Salvador, especially in the international arena. In his inaugural speech on 1 June 1984, Duarte said that he intended to "fight openly and tirelessly to control the abuse of authority and the violence of the extremes, the death-squads, and all the problems of injustice and power they represent." But international organisations refute this claim; in practice, Duarte's record shows that human rights violations, far from being eliminated, have instead become merely more selective. In 1985, more than 240 death-squad killings were tabulated by Tutela Legal, the human rights office of the Catholic Church, roughly equivalent to 1984 levels although greatly reduced from the levels of 1980–83.[19] An evaluation of Duarte's record by Amnesty International concludes:

> Since President José Napoleón Duarte assumed office in June 1984, Amnesty International has continued to receive reports of human rights violations, including arbitrary detentions, 'disappearances', individual death-squad killings and the extrajudicial execution of non-combatant civilians. Such violations, however, appear to be taking place on a more selective basis against people suspected of being in opposition to the present government or of being sympathetic to those that are. In response to expressions of international concern regarding human rights violations, a series of governments have blamed them on so-called death-squads, which Amnesty International has concluded to be made up of members of the Salvadorean security and military forces acting under the direct orders of superior officers.[20]

Although responsibility for the activities of the death-squads has been consistently linked to personnel of the Salvadorean army and security forces, to date no such personnel have been tried for the slaying of Salvadorean nationals.

Americas Watch notes that:

> Members of the Salvador armed forces, and particularly officers, who have engaged in death-squad killings, disappearances or the mass killing of civilians in the course of military operations face no prospect of punishment. Since it does not try to punish those responsible for such crimes, the government of El Salvador must be held accountable for committing such crimes as a matter of policy.[21]

We should not be shocked that the threat and the application of physical harm in El Salvador is bluntly used to frighten people into complying with government policies — the abuse of human rights is government policy. A September 1986 review of political prisoners conducted by the non-governmental Human Rights Commission of El Salvador (CDHES) found that 99.5% of the prisoners in La Esperanza jail had been subjected to "cruel, inhuman and degrading treatment" during detention.[22]

The torturers and the murderers are neither sick nor mad; they are trained. And the abuse of human rights is not a gruesome phenomenon characteristic of obscure and backward Third World countries, but rather one tactic in a strategy that has been designed

The torturers and murderers are neither sick nor mad; they are trained.

in cold blood to "draw the line" against the kind of change at stake in a country like El Salvador.

This policy affects everyone in every aspect of national life; the threat and the fear are ever-present, sometimes open, sometimes uneasily felt in the background or kept out by high walls and barbed wire. The effect is debilitating, and the victim of the policy is the nation itself. Appearances are deceptive, the unknown is not to be trusted and risks are not taken unavoidably.

A dramatic surge in the number of persons arbitrarily detained is but one of the causes of these symptoms. Most of the detainees are held for a limited period, usually two weeks, abused, intimidated and then released. In 1985, an estimated 25–30 people a week were abducted by government security forces.[23] In the first three months of 1986 CDHES recorded 596 detentions, almost 50 per week, of whom a total of only 61 were finally imprisoned. Detentions, combined with physical brutality, serve the clear political purpose of removing the leadership of groups perceived to oppose government policy, such as humanitarian organisations or trade unions, without causing the kind of international outcry which political assassinations attract. In particular, the number of detentions has had little impact, in the US Congress or elsewhere, on the levels of foreign aid Duarte is able to secure.

Activists are targeted for abduction, and tortured to extract confessions which incriminate them and the organisations they represent. This is of course in direct violation of the United Nations Declaration on Torture, which states in Article 12:

> Any statement which is established to have been made as a result of torture or other cruel, inhuman or degrading treatment may not be invoked as evidence against the person concerned or against any other person in any proceedings.

But in El Salvador, torture in unacknowledged detention is encouraged by the existence of legislation under the State of Siege, in effect with brief interruptions since 1980, which suspends the constitutional guarantees of citizens. Moreover, Decree Law 50, in force since February 1984, allows the security forces to hold a suspect incommunicado for up to 15 days, allows proceedings to be brought simply on the basis of unsubstantiated denunciations, and admits extra-judicial confessions as evidence.

A former Salvadorean Treasury policeman, interviewed on a British television documentary about torture, described in detail some of the inhuman practices he used against his government's opponents:

Q: The torture that you were present at — was putting people's heads in buckets of excrement, electrical torture . . .?

A: Oh, this is nothing . . .

Q: Did it get worse than that?

A: Electrical shocks — nobody will die unless it is too severe. But if you cut somebody — their skin — or you take somebody's eyes — this is actually what they did at the torture — with a pencil you take one eye out and you say, "If you don't talk I will take another one." And you say "I will pull your teeth out", and they do — one by one.

I don't know — do you want to hear all that? — you cut the fingers, you know why? Do you think this person will go alive after you cut a finger or you take their eyes or you destroy the ears with sound or with hitting this person in the ears — or when you take the organ of this person, the genital organ, you cut it — if a man you cut his organ?

This is the torture.

And this person bleeds to death, and then you laugh around him, drinking, smoking marijuana, using LSD, all kinds of drugs. And you feel bad after the torture takes place, after the person disappears — you throw the person away. You say 'This guy was hard to kill' — this is the conversation after the torture.

But in the torture you try to destroy this person physically — this is how they fight terrorists, Communists — to eliminate a person — this is it. They are trained to eliminate.

In the same documentary a former member of the Salvadorean National Guard was also interviewed:

Q: How many people did you torture? How many did you kill?

A: Well, as far as killing — there were about 2,000 people, and regarding to torture about 50 or 60.

Q: Is that you personally?

A: It wasn't only me. I belonged to a squad of twelve and we devoted ourselves to torture and to finding people we were told were guerrillas.

Q: What type of training did you receive?

A: I was trained in Panama by the Red Berets of the United States in guerrilla warfare. Part of the time we were instructed about torture and part of the time we were taught self-defence.[24]

According to the investigations of international organisations such as Americas Watch, which has a researcher permanently based in El Salvador and produces two highly regarded reports per year, human rights violations have recently become both more selective and more subtle. Mistreatment of detainees is still common, but the methods of torture employed tend to be those that leave fewer physical marks. This does not make them any the less effective, nor any more humane. Methods most commonly reported include the *capucha*, an airtight hood – often impregnated with lime — which is held over the victim's head repeatedly to the point of suffocation; immersion in tanks of excrement; food and sleep deprivation; and threats against family members. The security forces appear to have become convinced at least of the need to keep prisoners alive in order to gather intelligence information which can be used in the war effort. But beatings, electric shocks and rape are also reported to be on the increase.[25]

CDHES produced a remarkable study of political prisoners when a number of their own workers were detained and spent several months in La Esperanza prison in the capital, San Salvador. They investigated all 434 prisoners remanded from January to August 1986, and identified 40 principal techniques of torture that had been applied to the victims: all but two of the prisoners had been subjected to some form of torture, and many had experienced several different types — 19 of the 40 tortures were used on half or more of the victims. In at least one case, US personnel were said to have been present during the interrogation and torture sessions.[26]

United States involvement in El Salvador extends to complicity in human rights abuses. US advisers train the Salvadorean security forces in interrogation techniques in Panama and in the US; in August 1986, for example, three high-ranking officers of the National Guard participated in a US-funded training programme at a police academy in Phoenix, Arizona, according to a CBS TV report.

CBS quoted a Democrat Senator as saying: "They're training hard-core killers to be more efficient, perhaps to be even better at their job. We sort of gave them the cloak of legitimacy by bringing them here. I tell you, it is just despicable."[27]

One widely reported torture case has particularly disturbing implications of US involvement. Graciela Menéndez de Iglesias, a 32-year-old USAID employee and an economist fluent in English, was arrested at the US Embassy by US officials and illegally interrogated before being handed over to the Treasury Police, where she was subsequently tortured. Following her detention in September and October 1985 she fled the country, and was interviewed in exile by a reporter for *The Sunday Times*:

[Menéndez] was interrogated for four hours in the embassy by four American security agents who told her that if she did not 'collaborate' they would use 'all their power' to destroy her. The Americans wanted a list of alleged guerrilla infiltrators in the embassy. Menéndez, who protested her innocence throughout, was unable to help them.

After the interrogation, Menéndez was handed over, at the embassy gates, to the Treasury Police. She was detained at their headquarters for a further 15 days. *Sunday Times* inquiries confirm that she was raped repeatedly during her detention, kept blindfolded, often completely naked and, during relentless interrogation sessions, was made to stand with her arms in the air. The Treasury Police kept her awake with drugs and jets of cold water.

During her detention by the Treasury Police, she was interrogated and threatened on three occasions by American security agents, who told her: 'We pay the bills. We have a lot of power.'

One agent told her she could be kept in the Treasury Police cell for 15 days, then given life imprisonment or made to "disappear" if she did not provide the information they wanted: "This is my speciality. I'm an expert at dealing with terrorists", he told her.

The embassy acknowledges that 'at the request of the Salvadorean authorities', US officials did question Menéndez at police headquarters.[28]

Subsequently, the United States also acknowledged that it was aware of allegations of mistreatment of Menéndez, but denied that it was in any way involved. Assistant Secretary for Inter-American Affairs, Elliott Abrams, declared in a letter to the *Sunday Times*: "I believe her story to be a fabrication." But according to Americas Watch, it was Abrams who in his letter of denial "made false and misleading statements."[29] These events occurred in the context of the lifting of a Congressional ban on US training of foreign police forces, which had been imposed in the mid-1970s following charges that the US AID Public Safety Program had trained police who systematically tortured prisoners. In mid-1985, Congress granted exemptions to El Salvador, and $4.8 million is currently allocated for training programmes for the National Police, the National Guard and the Treasury Police, which will be run by US advisers.[30]

From January 1987, Britain is for the first time providing training for Salvadorean military forces. A single cadet is currently receiving instruction at Sandhurst, where the British government alleges that he will be exposed to the 'civilising' influence of the British military tradition. So far, it is no more than a gesture, but what is significant is what the gesture is saying; for it signifies the establishment of concrete links between the UK and the Salvadorean military, and the turning of a blind eye to reports of continuing and systematic violations of human rights by the army in El Salvador.

PART FOUR

The Silenced Majority

12
A Solution Among Salvadoreans

The targets of the death-squads and the detentions are primarily leaders and members of labour and peasant organisations, religious groups (particularly those working with the displaced), socially deprived sectors such as the displaced themselves, and teacher and student activists. These sectors of Salvadorean society make up what may be broadly termed the 'popular movement': that is, civilian groups who share a common demand for real structural change in their country.

It is not an organised political movement as such, but rather the convergence around a minimum programme which unites a diversity of political tendencies. The popular movement has a history which goes back a long way in El Salvador — a long history of resistance and repression. Similar groups to those which opposed the military dictatorships now oppose what they themselves describe as the façade of democracy under Duarte, and they suffer similar reprisals.

At the current stage of the struggle, they unite to demand a negotiated solution to the war, which they insist must take into account the issues which have generated the conflict, in order to end the suffering of the nation.

"Diálogo Si — Guerra No!" ("Yes to Dialogue — No to War") is a rallying cry that has brought together a broad diversity of groups, including former government supporters, to press for a resolution of the country's problems. They protest that the war is bleeding the country dry, that the course of the fighting has shown that neither side has the short- or even long-term prospect of defeating the other militarily. The guerrillas have been able to take everything the military bonanza of the middle 1980s has thrown at them, but so long as that machine is maintained they cannot mount an offensive that could overturn it. The continuation of the fighting in these circumstances will be of benefit to no one inside El Salvador: it will only accelerate the destruction of the country, perhaps beyond the point of recovery.

The fear underlying all other fears is that the US has shown itself to be so hostile to the idea of independent change in Central America, and so determined to maintain its control, that a revolutionary victory would in any case attract more problems than it could hope to solve.

This is an important point. The demand for dialogue is an attempt to take the Salvadorean conflict out of the power plays of external protagonists, and to put its resolution back into the hands of the people themselves. It is, of course, a compromise, but, under the circumstances, not an unreasonable one. The revolution would inherit a country shattered by conflict, and undoubtedly would face an immediate counter-revolutionary attack, draining the resources it could devote to development, as is the case in Nicaragua.

Stripped to its essentials, the name of the game now is to seek a formula that the United States will find, perhaps not acceptable, but difficult to reject: a solution among Salvadoreans.

Negotiations are even more difficult for Duarte to reject, since they are demanded by a clear majority of the people. Traditionally, the will of the people has not amounted to a political imperative in El Salvador, but the course of the war has meant that they have learned to construct and to defend new mechanisms of expression. Political space under the Duarte regime is limited, but what does exist has been exploited to the full. And the war itself has exacted so high a cost that the people make their demands not as requests, but as necessities.

Most significantly, the mobilisation of such diverse sectors to demand talks implies a condemnation of Duarte's role. The strongest voice has come from the organised labour movement, and includes significant sectors of the Christian Democrats' own party base. Those who had hopes of a 'moderate alternative' and who believed the promises Duarte made — those who delivered the votes on election day — have since been pushed into opposition by government policies which have catered to the interests of the United States, the military and the businessmen. Even these beneficiaries are not at all happy with the results they have got. In the meantime, the real cost of the war is being paid with the blood and hunger of the poor: the peasants, the displaced, the unemployed; even those who do have jobs are living an increasingly marginal and dispossessed existence.

Despite the $2 million per day of US aid, Duarte's government has brought no improvements to the lives of the overwhelming

The peasants, the displaced, the unemployed and even those who have jobs are living an increasingly marginal and dispossessed existence.
San Salvador slum.

majority of Salvadoreans; on the contrary, their conditions have worsened drastically. While the bombs and the bullets fly, the economy has been kept alive by inputs of foreign aid which merely allow national resources to be diverted to feed the war, so that directly or indirectly the dollars go to pay for the fighting — not to stimulate investment or production or to create jobs. The effect is to feed the country's external debt, which further undermines the economy. El Salvador's debt in 1984 was $2,300 million, accounting for 60% of the 1983 Gross Domestic Product; servicing that debt in 1985 consumed 56% of the country's export earnings.[1]

Figures on economic performance in 1985, released by the country's Central Reserve Bank, show that per capita income had slumped to 1960 levels, while consumer prices have tripled since 1978.[2] In 1985, salaries declined in real value by more than 23%,[3] in the context of a rate of inflation that, by April 1986, exceeded 36%;[4] at the same time, out of every 100 of the economically active population only 35 actually hold regular employment.[5]

In January 1986, Duarte announced an economic "package" which halved the value of the currency and pushed up the prices of fuel, building and agricultural materials, medicines, public services and basic foodstuffs. The package was introduced under US pressure to shift a greater proportion of the cost of the war on to the Salvadorean economy, as the Reagan Administration came under fire from Congress to cut foreign aid expenditure and reduce its own vast federal fiscal deficit. Within El Salvador, the package restricted imports of fertilisers and other products essential to agricultural production, further contracting the economy and reducing employment and wages; following a brief freeze, prices of basic goods shot up dramatically. And since spending on the war cannot be reduced without jeopardising the government's position, the increased burden has again been borne by cuts in public employment and the shattered social services — that is, by the Salvadorean people.

It was in response to this package of measures that, in February 1986, the country was to see the formation of the broadest labour alliance ever assembled in El Salvador. The National Unity of Salvadorean Workers (UNTS) brought together an estimated half a million affiliated workers around a platform of demands that presented Duarte with the most serious political challenge of his presidency. The Popular Democratic Unity (UPD), once the backbone of the Christian Democrats' electoral machine, joined with the more radical unions of the First of May Committee, as well as other groups, to launch UNTS. The UPD argued that it had earlier supported Duarte only on the condition that he fulfil commitments to reform agreed to in the 1984 pre-election "Social Pact".[6] One of the UPD's former leaders pointed out that: "Two years ago I defended the Social Pact together with Duarte in this very *plaza*, and today I have come back here to denounce his failure to fulfil his promises, and to support the National Unity of Salvadorean Workers."

At the "Assembly for Survival" at which UNTS was launched, about 1,000 delegates from unions all over the country gathered in the square outside the Legislative Assembly and explained why they had come and what they wanted:

> These years of conflict have meant enormous losses for our country ... and the war doesn't show any sign of coming to an end; on the contrary, it becomes more profound. If this is not reversed, it will cause the total destruction of our people. Some governments, especially the United States, and some sectors in our own country are busy looking for a military victory; but they don't have anything to lose from the deterioration of the conflict because they don't need anything. They already have it all, and they are not the ones who go to fight — they are not the ones whose lives are at stake!
>
> In the face of this, the workers and the poor and humble must take the initiative, because we don't want to go on living with this war that is draining our blood. We want peace! But not peace with hunger and misery — we want peace with social justice .... It is clear that the war will not be won with more war.

The assembly adopted a common platform of demands that broadly oppose Duarte's economic and social policies, and it especially criticised the conduct of the war: it insisted on human rights guarantees and a halt to persecution, on the right of the displaced to be allowed to return to their homes, and on the people's demand for dialogue with the rebels — "in order to end the crisis and to free resources for development not war. Only then will it be possible to talk of a true peace."[7]

UNTS is independent of any political party, and yet these demands are clearly of a political nature and go to the heart of the failure of the US–Christian Democrat project in El Salvador. Less than two weeks after its foundation, UNTS was able to mobilise 100,000 supporters on a march in the capital — a show of popular force not seen for the previous six years.[8] It was in response to this pressure that Duarte announced, on 1 June 1986, that he would renew negotiations with the FDR–FMLN, stalled for a year and a half. The rebel political–military coalition had made several earlier proposals to reopen talks and had also made concessions on the

"We want peace! But not peace with hunger and misery — we want peace with social justice".

agenda, but it was the mass mobilisation of his own domestic constituency that forced Duarte towards the negotiating table.

This reveals the importance of the resurgent popular movement, of which UNTS is only the most dramatic example. The fundamental aim of the counterinsurgency plan was to create a sufficient level of support for the government to marginalise the rebel forces, and yet at the mid-point of his term Duarte has lost the whole of his popular support. His government faces unprecedented opposition to almost every aspect of its policies. The idea had been to create a limited political space which would be controlled by the Christian Democrats, using a careful mixture of selective repression and selective patronage — to give the illusion of just enough democracy.

The UPD itself was heavily funded by labour organisations in the United States, the AFL–CIO and its international arm, the American Institute for Free Labour Development (AIFLD). Many of its leaders were given jobs in the PDC government; but intrigue and manipulation by the US organisations, coupled with the failure of the PDC to implement significant reform, eventually caused the disintegration of the organisation. Over 90% of AIFLD's budget is paid by USAID, and its objectives have been closely identified with US government policy. After the launch of UNTS, AIFLD officials worked hard to pressure the UPD to withdraw its participation, and one leader we spoke to told us how he had himself been offered money and a new car, as well as finance and a building for his union, if he would pull out of UNTS:

> They read me the letter which I was to sign to pull out, in which they also offered money to pay for a congress to make the announcement: they were going to pay for each person to attend. But I answered that we had already held a national assembly in which we decided to join UNTS, and that the grassroots had made the decision to join; I said that I was not a leader of my stomach but a leader of my people.

In the end, the UPD did withdraw from the UNTS alliance, but it left behind a number of its constituent organisations who preferred to continue to work in the context of unity that had been achieved. What fell away was a divided shell; and what remained was still the largest labour grouping in the country's history. The point to be drawn from this is that a popular movement cannot be overcome simply by buying off its leaders, at least when the political development of the people the movement represents is at an advanced stage, as is certainly the case in El Salvador.

It is worth remembering that in El Salvador, political parties anywhere to the left of the Christian Democrats were in practice outlawed by the slaughter of the 1979–83 period. Even before those dark years, the formal political process was manipulated by the military through fraud and violence. It is in this sense that the majority of the people in the country have always been excluded from political participation: in the great 'democratic experiment' which brought Duarte to power, the choice had been between the Christian Democrats and the far right, whose leader, Roberto d'Aubuisson, was described by a former US Ambassador to El Salvador as "a pathological killer" and who has been closely linked to the death-squads.

Political demands have long been expressed directly through grassroots organisations such as those which make up the spectrum of the popular movement. In the climate of severe repression of the 1980s what happened was that political work became concentrated at base level, among the individual workers at a factory or the residents of a poor neighbourhood, to avoid the targeting of leaders for assassination. As a result, the popular movement as a whole has become much more difficult to crush or co-opt.

Union members have developed a degree of independence from their leaders, so that it is not enough to "disappear" the general secretary or offer him a car or a government job. The result is an extremely sophisticated level of organisation, and Salvadorean unions today represent a mature, powerful social and political force. The people can make up their own minds; if Duarte has not delivered his promises, if they see in their own lives that the situation in the country is intolerable, they can take their organisation with them into opposition — and they have done so. UNTS is to this extent a direct response to continuing repression and to other recent government measures such as the outlawing of strikes in the public sector, and the militarisation of the workplaces to deal with industrial action.

The strength of the popular movement lies precisely in the fact that its unity is founded on principles of ideological pluralism: it acts at the level of consensus and retains the right and the capacity to determine its own programme. It is not merely the voice of any single political entity, although its constituent groups may have their own, often opposing, allegiances. It is more than the sum of its parts.

Agreement between such diverse groups is always difficult to maintain. In many conversations we had with unionists we heard them stress the importance of avoiding ideological confrontations

The people can make up their own minds.

with other sectors of the union movement. In a single room that acts as headquarters for one of the largest left-wing unions, Gustavo, a labour leader with years of bitter experience and wisdom etched in the lines around bright eyes piercing his leathery face, told us that unity was an overriding need within the political context of El Salvador:

> We have been involved with all of the union federations which the United States has created. We believe that we shouldn't pay much attention to who the directors of the organisation are because their policies come from abroad; what we are concerned about, and what we are obliged to defend, are the interests of the workers wherever they are. So in this way we march together with all of these organisations . . . .
>
> And they are also fighting with us, because they know the real situation in our country. We have had so many people, so many leaders and brave ones, who have fallen at the hands of the police and the repressive security forces, that the people have developed a political consciousness regardless of the ideology of the organisation to which they belong. Sooner or later we will all find ourselves in the same position, one that will bring us together to forge a real and lasting peace, and to win too a series of demands that the stomachs of the people dictate.

The government response to the formation of UNTS was immediate and predictable: Duarte unsuccessfully tried to ban the venue for the "Assembly for Survival"; subsequently, the army public relations office said that the organisation had been "infiltrated", a clear warning to its leaders; at a Mayday rally soon afterwards the demonstrators were buzzed by military helicopter overflights; and AIFLD claimed that the alliance was "a secret campaign to create problems for Duarte, organised by the guerrillas using union collaborators" — in El Salvador not a charge to be taken lightly.[9]

Duarte quickly put together his own "umbrella" coalition, the National Peasant–Worker Union (UNOC), made up from the leftovers of the UPD. Whereas peasants from the rural areas who attempted to travel to the UNTS Mayday rally had been prevented from reaching the capital, UNOC supporters were bussed in for a pro-government march using state vehicles and fuel, causing vitriolic protests from right-wing opposition parties alleging abuse of government privileges.[10]

In the light of his record so far, Duarte's chances of defeating UNTS and the resurgent popular movement in a straight fight look slim, and he stands to lose even more credibility if he fails. Increased levels of human rights violations during 1986 as the government tried to counter the resurgent popular movement have already undermined his credibility on the international scene. And at the same time, the fragile unity of the union coalition has been reinforced in the face of attack by what is now the common enemy.

Moreover, by getting its members out on to the streets, by marching to demand peace, by specifying what kind of peace and how it should be achieved, the popular movement has taken the initiative into its own hands at the current stage of the war. At the Mayday 1986 rally UNTS leaders said: "We are not only going to force a dialogue to take place, we want to participate in that dialogue, representing the social majority of the country."[11]

The first meeting for negotiations between President Duarte and the rebel FDR–FMLN coalition took place in October 1984, in La Palma, a small town in Chalatenango province. It was seen by all, nationally and internationally, as an historic encounter. Duarte, who had announced his willingness to hold talks in front of the General Assembly of the United Nations, was hailed as a peace-maker. Within El Salvador, people of all political persuasions hung white flags from their windows and balconies and flocked to the venue for the talks in a spontaneous demonstration of national consensus. It was an optimistic time, and inside the rebel-controlled northern Morazán province I listened eagerly to the radio reports from La Palma with a column of equally excited guerrilla fighters who were guarding the river crossing.

During the severest years of repression the government had called on the rebels to lay down their arms and take part in elections, even though international observers reported that the electoral process did not provide adequate guarantees for the participation of the left.[12] And in the event, Duarte's position at the La Palma talks was little different. The rebels proposed a ceasefire, formation of a government of national conciliation and fusion of the two armies leading to elections in which the free participation of all parties would be guaranteed, but all that was actually agreed was that the process of negotiation should continue. There was a second meeting in November, following which the talks broke down because of the lack of agreement over a basic agenda: one of the key sticking points was the government's insistence that the negotiations be held outside the country.

Throughout 1985, the FDR–FMLN made several proposals to set a date for a third round of talks, but all were rejected by the Duarte Administration. The guerrillas suggested that if the government halted the influx of military aid from the United States, they too would cut off the supplies they have always been alleged to receive from abroad; they also offered to halt economic sabotage if the government stopped the escalating aerial bombardments of rural areas.[13] But the dialogue remained stalled in the face of bitter opposition from the right and from the military, who feared concessions to the guerrillas, and amid accusations from the popular movement that Duarte had no serious intention of undertaking concrete negotiations.

Gustavo told us of the frustration he felt at the government's lack of sincerity and progress in the talks:

> We think of peace as a means to resolve our basic needs, a process which truly solves our problem. This can only be achieved through a negotiated political solution, a sincere dialogue between the opposing sides . . . .
>
> But Duarte tells us to keep quiet, to suffer what is happening and stoically support the government. What we have seen is that he has announced his intention to hold talks in front of the United Nations, and then just asked the other side to surrender. This is not possible, and everyone here knows it . . . .
>
> We want peace — but not the peace of the cemetery, and not the peace of being silenced.

In 1986, however, the pace of events overtook the government: Duarte found himself on the defensive, pressured by many groups, including some who could not just be dismissed as "subversives", to renew talks.[14] UNTS and other labour federations, including pro-government organisations, joined with small businessmen, the church, religious groups, students, the displaced and more. That this should happen so soon after the years of wholesale repression in which opposition movements were thought to have been crushed is remarkable.

The key psychological element of the counterinsurgency drive was undercut because people saw the government as being interested only in continuing an unpopular war. Duarte has been unable to come up with any realistic alternative to negotiations as a way of bringing the war to an end.

In June, Duarte capitulated and announced he was willing to hold a third round of talks; but he did not regain the political initiative. In the weeks before the meeting was to take place, groups throughout the country held their own meetings, proposing their own demands and their own agenda for the talks in a national dialogue played out to a considerable degree in public.

Duarte has been unable to come up with any realistic alternative to negotiations as a way of bringing the war to an end.

A few basic points are common to most analyses: that it is not possible to return to the past and that the political process must be opened to those traditionally excluded; that a solution is essential in order to end the suffering of the people and the destruction of the country; and that the need for peace must override the narrow interests of each side, who should make compromises to secure agreement.[15]

The public argument went further: increasingly, organisations demanded the right to participate directly in the negotiations, since Duarte is perceived to represent only one side of the social divide.[16] The government's credibility is at an all time low. Even its own worker–peasant creation, UNOC, which was designed to oppose the UNTS labour alliance, insisted on the presence of workers' representatives at the talks.[17]

The right was left without a viable argument. The National Association of Private Enterprise (ANEP), which represents big business interests, was left claiming that the constitution allows 'dialogue' only through the electoral process, so that negotiations over power-sharing would be unconstitutional. The Catholic Church immediately responded that if the constitution was an obstacle, it should be changed.

Archbishop Rivera pushed the point home: "It is not the law that makes man," he said, "but man that makes the law."[18]

And an earlier pastoral letter from El Salvador's bishops warned, "If the dialogue fails, the only alternative open to El Salvador will be destruction."[19]

Right-wing political parties found that opposition to negotiations was no longer a realistic policy, and tried to build an alternative alliance between private business interests and the Army; but they, too, failed to offer any new proposals, merely arguing for continuing support for military efforts to "break the will of the terrorists to fight, and force them to take the channels of the democratic process."[20]

It was in the context of this national debate that the military launched its solution to the conflict: "United to Reconstruct", the new pacification plan, which threateningly called on all sectors to "drop our personal, group or party positions, and unite to defend the national interest."[21]

It was at this time too that the government stepped up attacks on humanitarian groups and popular organisations.[22]

FDR–FMLN negotiators proposed that all political groups and parties who wished to participate in the negotiations should be invited to the next stage of the talks, causing a good deal of embarrassment to the President when this proposal was welcomed by groups from both the left and right.[23] They also offered to hold a televised debate with Duarte and army commanders to discuss the conduct of the war.

As the pressure mounted within the country it seemed less and less likely that the government could afford to go to a meeting. The rector of the Central American University pointed out that:

> the government is limited in its capacity to negotiate by the fact that the US Embassy, the Armed Forces, the right-wing and certain media interests do not want a political solution to the conflict.[24]

By this time the third round was already doubtful; a preliminary agreement to hold the meeting in the small eastern town of Sesori, chosen because it was not held by either side, was followed by the immediate occupation of the site by the elite counterinsurgency Arce battalion.

In the meantime, Duarte stated publicly that the only agreement he would accept from the rebels would be to lay down their arms,[25] and he confirmed that the military occupation of Sesori would be indefinite, claiming that the army presence was necessary "to ensure the security" of the delegates.[26]

This ensured that the talks were aborted: the rebels were unwilling to place the security of their delegates in army hands and the meeting never took place. In Sesori on the appointed day, Duarte delivered a monologue on peace to some 2,000 state employees bussed in for the occasion, a gesture condemned by all sides as a waste of petrol and a cheap publicity attempt.

Nevertheless, a form of national dialogue had been debated within the country in this period between June and September; and remarkably, a considerable degree of consensus had been reached.

Almost immediately afterwards the earthquake struck, providing a macabre distraction from the government's internal crisis. The natural disaster, which killed 1,000 and left 200,000 homeless overnight, and which left behind a bill for $2 billion, reinforced all the arguments for negotiations.

As the Air Force continued to fly its bombing runs on villages in the Salvadorean countryside in the days following the tragedy, the absurdity was obvious to all.

The Catholic Church called on the community of nations to:

> unite our forces — not only to overcome the destruction caused by this natural catastrophe, but to resolve the greater tragedy of the war whose solution depends on human decisions . . . .[27]

13
Self-Help

Civilians in El Salvador are not passive victims of the conflict that has cost them so dearly. The course of the war has shown that they will not give up in the face of personal or collective disaster. Even the most destitute retain their dignity and their capacity to seek their own solutions.

Many of those we accompanied on the March for Peace in January 1986 were peasant families discarded by their society to life in the slums and shanty-towns; yet they have the courage to confront those who have power over them.

In July, in response to the death threats levelled against church humanitarian workers, these people, who themselves face a daily oppression, held a vigil in the Metropolitan Cathedral to demonstrate in public their support for the priests and nuns who had risked their lives to help them. One explained:

> You see, they gave us support, and helped us to have food to eat and a roof over our heads. If it is for this that they are going to be killed, if for holding out a hand to us they will be murdered, then we, the displaced, want to be at their side.[28]

Like other groups not represented by the political system in El Salvador, the displaced have created their own organisations to press their demands: for the right to return to their homes and for negotiations to halt the bombings and the militarisation of the areas they have been forced to abandon. They have marched to the presidential palace many times to present these demands, and when they have received no reply they have organised their own resettlement projects with the help of national and international humanitarian agencies. In the context of the programmes designed by counterinsurgency strategists in Washington and elsewhere, the initiatives of these groups, such as the Christian Committee for the Displaced (CRIPDES) and the National Coordinating Committee for Repopulation (CNR), are particularly significant because these are the response of the 'victims' themselves to the problems they face.

CRIPDES was formed in 1984 when a group of displaced people living in the marginal areas of the capital came together at a church in the city centre, and discovered that they all shared similar conditions and difficulties. They decided to carry out their own investigation of the issue at national level, and then formed the Committee which quickly grew to represent the majority of the displaced. They were clear about their objectives from the beginning: they saw that the situation of the uprooted population was producing dependency and hopelessness among the people, and that a resettlement programme was needed urgently to give them back the chance to work and to produce for themselves. We spoke to some of the elected leaders of the group, themselves displaced people, in one of the church refugee centres, crowded and with children running in every direction, since the organisation doesn't have the funds to run an office of its own:

> The difference between CRIPDES and government aid organisations like CONADES[29] is that these organisations are not created to serve the people but to serve political objectives, to monopolise for their own political ends the international aid destined for the displaced . . . .
>
> These are tactics used by the government as part of a pacification strategy, not for the benefit of the people themselves. CRIPDES was not formed by anyone — we are the displaced, and we saw the need to organise ourselves so that we would not be manipulated by others. This is a problem that we have with the authorities. When we began to grow and to make our own demands the government became afraid that we would be a problem, since we were demanding our rights . . . .
>
> Because the displaced have no freedom. Those who organise to take care of the needs of a community do so always with the fear that they may be threatened or persecuted for their meetings and actions. The authorities want to have control over the work that we do . . . .
>
> What we want as people who have been uprooted is to be able to return to our homes; but we are aware that we cannot live in the places we come from so long as the war goes on — it is because of the indiscriminate bombings and because of the mortars and the army operations that we have had to flee these areas.

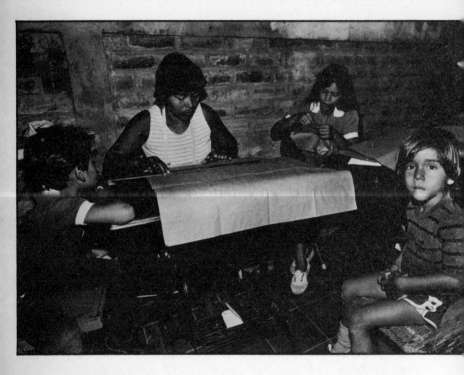

The response of the 'victims' themselves to the problems they face. Community-based sewing workshop provides skills which will enable the people to survive in the cities.

So we demand a peace in which we will be free to speak, a peace in which the people will make their own decisions: a just peace.

We don't want to go on being victims: until this peace comes, we are creating our own networks of production and supply.

In 1985 CRIPDES organised the first self-help attempt to resettle a group of displaced people from the San Salvador refuges to a pilot project on the south-eastern coast, in Usulután province. About 60 families left the capital in June and built simple houses, planted crops, and organised a small school and health clinic. But by September CRIPDES workers and members were facing obstruction from the army:

We began to take in aid to the resettlement, food and medicines, and to carry out pastoral and literacy work. But when the army realised this they began to check on us and they accused all the people there of being terrorists. The people are there because they know that in the city they might starve to death, while there at least there is some land to work and they can fish to survive with their families. But the army insists, in accordance with their military objectives, that these people should leave. They don't care whether the people will die of hunger, or that the people don't want this war . . . .

We went with a CRIPDES delegation to the coast to bring food to the project, but we were stopped by the army and taken to the barracks and held by them there; they refused to let us pass. We were detained for 20 hours, and interrogated all through the night. Then they broke open all of the packages of food, and when they didn't find anything with which to accuse us they took us back to San Salvador under a military escort. And since then we haven't been able to go back to the resettlement with food. Even the Red Cross has been forbidden to go there with supplies.

We also spoke to three catechists (lay religious workers) from the Usulután resettlement who had had to leave because of the danger they were facing in their work. They told us what happened during one of the army's periodic invasions of the project:

They came and took out the literacy teacher and the health worker from the clinic — these are small clinics which the people have built up with their own efforts. The soldiers took away all of the medicines . . . .

What they say is that it is the guerrillas who have given us this work to do; they asked the teacher who had told him to teach literacy classes, and when he said that the people had asked him themselves, they said he was a liar and that he was only teaching guerrillas ...

They were interrogating him there and they were beating him when he didn't give the answers they wanted; when he didn't accept what they were saying, they beat him. They also questioned the health worker in this way, and they confiscated all of the medicines. They left everything in a terrible mess. There were some boxes marked as donations from international humanitarian organisations, and the soldiers destroyed those ...

It is easy to see what they are trying to do. They want to wear the people down so that they will not be able to take any more and will leave; and in fact there are some families who have left because they were afraid. The people have just left refugee camps where they live shut up inside, and so they come hoping they will be able to find a new way of life and better conditions. They want to live like they did in the rural areas — but when they see that the army continues to persecute them they think that this is worse than staying in the camps ...

This is where our work is important, because after every time that the army comes we hold a Celebration of the Word [service] to try to keep up the spirit of the people; even though this is difficult because their suffering is very real.

It is not like sitting here just talking about what happens, because these people are living through all of these events.

These testimonies, like so many others we had listened to, brought home to us the fundamental impression of our visit, which was of people living through events and experiences that to us seemed intolerable, but that tó them were an unavoidable part of their lives, and of a process they were nevertheless determined to see through. Obstacles are continually being overcome because the people do not allow these obstructions to overcome them. The catechists we spoke to went back to Usulután to continue their work, and the displaced keep up their pressure to repopulate the destroyed lands of their country.

The process they are part of does not follow a direct course, but involves a commitment which enables people to adapt methods to the situation they are in. Take the case of Tenancingo for example; a small town just 20 miles from the capital, Tenancingo was abandoned in September 1983 after it was bombed and strafed by US-supplied A–37 jets from the Salvadorean air force, in an attack in which about 100 civilians were killed.[30] For more than two years it was a ghost town, like hundreds of others in El Salvador, its abandoned buildings no more than a crumbling memorial to the conflict. But its former residents did not disperse to the slums and the church centres which continue to absorb refugees fleeing similar experiences; instead, most of the people stayed together and maintained their community at a camp at a nearby town, with the help of a foreign aid worker. They formed a committee and appealed to the Catholic Church to support their demand to repopulate the town.

The key to the resettlement of Tenancingo was an unwritten agreement which the Archbishop was able to negotiate with care between the government and the guerrillas, that neither side would establish a permanent military presence in the town; in effect, Tenancingo was to become a demilitarised area in the middle of a war zone. In particular, the people were afraid that they would be forced to serve in the "civil defence" patrols that are at the core of the government rural pacification strategy. If it was off-limits to both sides, neither would have cause to attack the other in the town, the logic went, providing the necessary degree of security to the returning residents. This agreement had to be tacit since it implied recognition by the government of a duality of power in the country, and of the FMLN as a belligerent force, something strenuously denied in all official pronouncements. It was achieved only as a result of the personal pressure of Archbishop Rivera, who was described to us by one of the organisers as the "godfather" of the project.

The agreement was not the only thing about the project that makes the resettlement of Tenancingo unique. The repopulation was organised by FUNDASAL, a low-cost housing institute linked to the Catholic Church, and former residents were persuaded to waive their property rights, at least temporarily, so that those who wanted to return immediately would be able to occupy the buildings which were habitable, while FUNDASAL organised a second stage in which new houses would be constructed. The costs of the whole project were underwritten with considerable help from international non-governmental aid agencies, including Oxfam, Christian Aid and CAFOD (the Catholic Office for Overseas Development) in Britain.

Perhaps most important of all was the fact that one of the residents who pushed hardest for the deal was a landowner and also the richest man of the area. He was thus able to overcome problems of the extremes of wealth and poverty and the monopoly of land ownership in El Salvador that are at the root of the civil war. This is an important point, because any global schemes to deal with the question of those who have been uprooted by the war must deal also with the structural social and economic, and therefore political, inequalities which have generated the conflict.

The project as a whole is an exercise in diplomacy: the government and the army can point to Tenancingo as an example of their willingness to rebuild the country, even though the resettlement took place during the Phoenix Operation which depopulated the whole of the rest of the Guazapa area; while the guerrillas made a number of conditions for their agreement to observe the town's neutrality, including the banning of rapists and brothel-keepers, and prohibition of the collection of taxes or rents. And on 28 January 1986, we marched behind Monsignor Rivera with the first 56 families to return to Tenancingo to pick up the pieces of their lives.

Because of the factors which make it a unique experiment, this is not a model that will be easy to duplicate elsewhere. Nevertheless it is a milestone of sorts, since its complex compromises were made possible in the first place by the determination of the residents to return to their homes. Since the people went back army operations have continued in the surrounding area: on at least one occasion soldiers entered the town, searching houses and shooting indiscriminately in an incident in which one unarmed civilian was killed and a number of settlers detained, though later released.[31] In May, the elite *Batallón Belloso* was quartered in the town for several days, accompanying General Blandón, himself a native of Tenancingo, who proclaimed himself the town's protector "inasmuch as it is the Army that guarantees the peace of the resettlement",[32] and predicted ominously that the military would not tolerate "a town without authority."[33]

Other resettlements have been attempted since the repopulation of Tenancingo: CRIPDES launched a new coordinating group (the CNR) in May 1986 and in June announced through paid advertisements in the press that they intended to lead resettlements in two areas: the town of San José de las Flores in Chalatenango province, and Aguacayo, a village near the town of Suchitoto in the Guazapa region. Unlike the Tenancingo project, these resettlements were entirely organised by the displaced themselves, although they requested the support of the Church, the government and the army.

The people who were going back had been evacuated by force during military operations earlier in the year.[34] The CNR wrote to President Duarte to inform him of their intentions and to seek the government's permission to go back, but when they received no reply they decided to proceed with their initiative without official help. They argued that they could not wait any longer because they had to arrive in time to plant the crops they would need to survive.

As a precaution, the CNR invited a delegation of 22 foreign religious representatives, mostly from the United States, to accompany them on the difficult journey back to their homes, in order to provide some guarantee for the safety of the returnees. At a press conference held before the first convoy of buses set out for Chalatenango, this delegation explained why they felt it necessary to go back with the people:

> We believe that it is the role which our government plays in the supply of monies, materials, equipment, training and more than 100 advisors that actually makes possible the war of the Salvadorean government against its civilian population.
>
> Therefore, as citizens of the United States, we feel a responsibility not just to protest against the policies of our government, but also to try to relieve the effects of those policies.[35]

After a number of halts at military road-blocks, in which all the people were photographed and their identities carefully listed by the army, most of the families were able to get through to San José. A month later the same delegation accompanied the second group of returnees back to Aguacayo. Many of the 132 peasant families in this second group had been dislodged some months before during Operation Phoenix and had consistently pressured the authorities to allow them to go back, even mounting a hunger strike in one of the church refuges to which they had been sent. Now they were taking matters into their own hands as they set off in a convoy of ten buses and six trucks loaded with supplies. Teachers of the Jesuit University travelling with the group commented ironically:

> We couldn't resist copying a newspaper report here which described the journey back to Aguacayo:
>
> "Peasants who since February have fled from the terrorists from various villages in the area around Suchitoto, and have since stayed in refugee camps, yesterday returned to their places of origin under the protection of the authorities. They indicated that they were happy to go back to their homes, but that they were afraid they might again become victims of the terrorists at any moment if they could not rely on the constant vigilance of the Armed Forces." [*El Diario de Hoy*, 16/7/86.]
>
> The truth is exactly the opposite, but this is how they write the history of our country — without truth and without shame.[36]

The difficult journey back to their homes.

The hypocrisy of the official version was compounded by the events that were to follow. The people were detained in Aguacayo by a military patrol which refused to let them continue to their destination, a cooperative about an hour's walk further on; in the empty and abandoned village a lieutenant warned them:

> each and every one of the houses that you see here has an owner, and nobody likes to have what he has had to buy usurped by others. In a democracy you have to respect private property. We live in a democratic country in which the fundamental principle is private property . . . .[37]

In the face of this unanswerable argument, the expedition of more than 600 unarmed civilians decided to stay overnight in and around the bombed shell of the village church of Aguacayo.

The following day they celebrated a mass in the open air as they prepared to leave; but before they could set off they were again surrounded by a large contingent of soldiers who arrived in a convoy of trucks. The regional commander, Colonel Hernández, ordered all the foreigners to leave within half an hour, claiming they were breaking the law by entering a military area without permission. He announced that things were going to be sorted out amongst Salvadoreans, referring to the delegation as interlopers.

The priests and nuns were shocked and refused to leave the refugees, whom they had come to protect; they sat down in a circle, joined hands and began to sing "We Shall Overcome" and "Amazing Grace".[38] As they were singing they were lifted into the army trucks in scenes echoing the protest days of Vietnam, but this time in the more sinister setting of the charred countryside of El Salvador. They were taken to the military barracks at Suchitoto and from there to the Treasury Police headquarters in the capital; the next day they were driven to the Guatemalan border and deported on the orders of President Duarte.

The reaction within El Salvador was bitter:

> This expulsion has caused an outrage here in the country; the foreign churchpeople came solely to help and to protect peasants who are defenceless. They came in peace and at no time advocated violence. They brought no arms, nor bombs, nor planes, nor helicopters, as others do; they brought only their concern for the peasants and their faith in God. The declarations by the government, the Army and the US Embassy that the law must be upheld have a cynical ring when the millions of dollars for destruction are so warmly welcomed.[39]

One of the expelled US churchpeople offered his own conclusion: "democracy in El Salvador is a product of the imagination."[40]

Subsequently, of the 132 families who had set out to Aguacayo, 52 were again evicted by the Army; the others were able to remain, but a week later the Secretary of the cooperative was abducted by six heavily armed plain-clothesmen, and taken away in a polarised-glass vehicle. A few days after this two members of the National Coordinating Committee for Repopulation (CNR) were also 'disappeared'.

All these events are part of a story that doesn't yet have a conclusion. In the course of our investigation we spent a great deal of time with displaced people and with the priests of the progressive sectors of the church who carry on endless grassroots work with the silenced majority of El Salvador; it seems appropriate therefore that we should give one of those priests the last word in this book:

If this war ends, all depends on what kind of solution it ends with.

You must start from the fact that this country is divided: between a poor majority that wants justice and a rich minority that wants profit.

So if the minority continue to dominate at the end of the war, the people, who have committed themselves to the idea of a radical change of the system, will feel a deep frustration. They will have to go on living in subjection.

This will have sociological and economic consequences: people will feel dislocated, living in fear and fleeing persecution; and they will not be able to go back to the land to work and enjoy the fruits of their labour.

This means that the root problem of injustice and the war requires a change in the system as a whole, in such a way that these people will be able to rebuild their lives in an atmosphere of justice and freedom.

As long as there is no normality here — as there is not, despite claims of democratisation — any return to abandoned lands or any collective projects are conditioned by the actual atmosphere of terror which exists. This is not an exaggeration or a dramatisation. This is the reality that we see demonstrated daily: that there is no democracy, there is no freedom; the persecution and the murder, the detentions, the torture and the denunciations continue.

So resettlement projects are at present theoretical: it is not possible for people to return to abandoned lands without special measures on the part of humanitarian organisations to protect

"Nobody can hold power over a people who reject that power in an organised fashion."

them; otherwise, projects are designed by the army to make the people accept the conditions imposed by the existing system and its ideology, which deny their aspirations for freedom.

I believe that the displaced, as the fundamental victims of the war, can and must play a role as fighters for peace. Nobody can dispute their right to speak.

Our task is not simply to help make their situation bearable; we must help them to protest against their position.

I think that the system, and above all the repression it employs in its search for a military solution, cannot be maintained if the people organise themselves and do not permit it. Nobody can hold power over a people who reject that power in an organised fashion. The thing is to believe in them, to believe in the poor, in the people. If we believe in their capacity to act as agents in the transformation of history, then we have to work to help them organise to demand their own peace.

Notes

Part One: El Salvador In Brief (pp.1–26)

1. "El Salvador: The Struggle for Peace and Freedom", Report of the Labour Movement Delegation to El Salvador, London, 1986, p.10.

2. Gettleman, M.E., P. Lacefield, L. Menashe, D. Mermelstein, R. Radosh, *El Salvador in the New Cold War*, Grove Press, New York, 1981, p.35.

3. *Washington Post*, 9 September 1981.

4. Kwitny, Jonathan, "Tarnished Report? Apparent Errors Cloud US White Paper on Reds in El Salvador", *Wall Street Journal*, 6 June, 1981.

5. Ibid.

6. "Duarte: Prisoner of War", North American Congress on Latin America (NACLA), New York, January/March 1986, p.15.

7. Galeano, Eduardo, *Open Veins of Latin America*, Monthly Review Press, New York, 1973, p.121: "The day is not far distant when three Stars and Stripes at three equidistant points will mark our territory: one at the North Pole, one at the Panama Canal, and one at the South Pole. The whole hemisphere will be ours in fact as, by virtue of our superiority of race, it already is ours morally."

8. *El Salvador in the New Cold War*, op. cit., p.36.

9. Kornbluh, Peter and John Hackle, "Low-intensity Conflict", NACLA, New York, June 1986, p.10.

10. Wallace, Scott, "Contras Supplier May Be Tried"; and "Capture of Contra Ally is Lever for Sandinistas", *The Independent* (London), 9 and 10 October 1986, respectively.

11. *Hard Lessons*, NUT/WUS Delegation to El Salvador, WUS, London, 1986, p. 5 — citing Lord Chitnis' report for the Parliamentary Human Rights Group, March 1982.

12. Thomson, Marilyn, *Women of El Salvador*, Zed Books Ltd, London, 1986: Appendix 4 by Mandy Macdonald, p. 145.

13. NACLA, "Duarte Prisoner of War", op. cit., p. 15.

14. McClintock, Michael, *The American Connection*, Vol. 2, Zed Books Ltd, 1985, p. 302: Socorro Jurídico (Christian Legal Aid) findings for 1981 estimated 13,352 deaths resulting from political repression.

15. NACLA, "Duarte: Prisoner of War", op. cit., p. 16.

16. Ibid., p. 17.

17. "José Napoleón Duarte", *Playboy*, June 1984, p. 73.

18. *Torture in El Salvador*, El Salvador Human Rights Commission (CDHES), San Salvador, September 1986, p.26.

19. *Proceso*, No. 218, UCA, El Salvador, December 1986, p. 1.

20. NACLA, "Duarte: Prisoner of War", op. cit., p. 22.

21. Ibid.

22. *Proceso*, op. cit., pp. 4–8.

23. NACLA, "Duarte: Prisoner of War", op. cit., p. 30.

24. Norton, Chris, "Contra Flights Show Who Runs El Salvador", *The Independent*, (London), 13 December 1986.

25. Sumner, Lieutenant Gen. Gordon (Ret.), "Negotiating with Marxists in Central America", address to International Security Council Forum, Washington DC, 21 March 1985.

Part Two: *The War Against Civilians (pp. 27-75)*

1. NACLA, "Duarte Prisoner of War", January/March 1986, p. 29.

2. For a more complete discussion of Archbishop Romero's homilies and of liberation theology read: Alas, Higinio, *El Salvador: Por qué la insurrección?*, Secretario Permanente de la Comisión para la Defensa de los Derechos Humanos en Centro América, Costa Rica, 1982, pp. 236–47; and Berryman, Philip, *The Religious Roots of Rebellion*, SCM Press, London, 1984.

3. The non-governmental Human Rights Commission of El Salvador gives estimates of 14,343 for 1980 and 16,537 for 1981.

4. Simon, Laurence and James Stephens Jr., *El Salvador Land Reform 1980–1: Impact Audit*, Oxfam America, 1982, p.2.

5. Berryman, Philip, op. cit., pp. 104–9.

6. Pearce, Jenny, *Promised Land*, Latin America Bureau, London, 1986, p.171.

7. For a more detailed discussion on the evolution of counter-insurgency in El Salvador see: McClintock, Michael, *The American Connection*, Vol.2, Zed Books Ltd, London, 1985.

8. *Carta a las Iglesias*, UCA, El Salvador, 16–31 October 1986.

9. *The Times*, 12 August 1985.

10. Hedges, Chris, *The Dallas Morning News*, 21 January 1985.

11. Central America Report, No. 28, "Not Our Civilians", London, May/June 1986, p.10.

12. Clements, Dr Charles, *Witness to War*, Fontana, London, 1985, pp.1–2.

13. *The Times*, 12 August 1986.

14. Testimonies from "Operation Phoenix", collected by Tutela Legal (human rights office of the Catholic Archdiocese of El Salvador), Christian Committee for the Displaced of El Salvador (CRIPDES) and the Central American Univeristy, Simeón Cañas of El Salvador: January 1986.

15. Figures given by CRIPDES.

16. Miller, Marjory, *Los Angeles Times*, 9 February, 1986.

17. *Inforpress*, 6 October 1986, p.4.

18. Testimony from "Operation Chavez", collected by the Bulletin of the Christian Base Communities in El Salvador, March 1986.

19. *Soldier of Fortune Magazine,* June 1984.

20. Waghelstein, Colonel John, "Post Vietnam Counterinsurgency Doctrine", *Military Review,* January 1985.

21. NACLA, "Preparing the Battlefield", April/May 1986, p.29.

22. For further discussion of US programmes in Vietnam see: Fitzgerald, Frances, *Fire in the Lake,* Vintanga, New York, 1973.

23. *New York Times,* "House Panel Criticised", 3 October 1971.

24. *Inforpress,* 13 February 1986.

25. *Proceso,* "Terrorismo", Centro Universitario de Documentación y Información, 23 April 1986, p.10.

26. Archbishop Rivera y Damas' homily of 12 January 1986.

27. Ibid.

28. See *El Salvador's Other Victims,* the Lawyers Committee for International Human Rights, New York, April 1984.

29. *Proceso,* UCA, December 1985.

30. Ibid.

31. Golden, Tim, *Miami Herald,* 15 December 1985.

32. Ornstein, Susan, *El Salvador: A Mercenary's View,* Fort Meyers News Press, 23 October 1983.

33. NACLA, "Duarte: Prisoner of War", January/March 1986, p.26.

34. Sarkesian, Sam, "Low-intensity Conflict: Concepts, Principles and Policy Guidelines", p.5. — cited in NACLA, "The Real War", April/May 1986, p.37.

Part Three: Government Against the People (pp.77–111)

1. *Carta a las Iglesias,* Central American University, March 1986.

2. This was taken from a confidential report by a human rights worker who was present in the camp during these events.

3. *El Salvador 1985: Desplazados y Refugiados,* Instituto de Investigaciones, Central American University, San Salvador, 1985.

4. Ibid., p.204.

5. *Estudios Centroamericanos,* Central American University, San Salvador, January/February 1986.

6. NACLA Report on the Americas, "The Real War", April/May 1986.

7. *El Salvador Briefing,* May 1986.

8. *El Salvador Briefing,* January 1986.

9. Whagelstein, Colonel John, "Post-Vietnam Counterinsurgency Doctrine", *Military Review,* January 1985.

10. *El Salvador's Other Victims,* Lawyers Committee for International Human Rights, New York, April 1984.

11. See Chapter 8.

12. *El Salvador Briefing,* September 1986.

13. *El Salvador Briefing,* August and September 1986.

14. Tutela Legal, Informe No. 43, November 1985.

15. "Laura Pinto speaks", *New Statesman,* 18 July 1986.

16. *Inforpress Centroamericano,* 10 July 1986.

17. Ibid.

18. *Settling Into Routine,* Human Rights Abuses in Duarte's Second Year,

Americas Watch, New York, May 1986, p.124.
19. Ibid., pp.39–43.
20. Amnesty International Urgent Action, UA326/85, 22 November 1985.
21. Americas Watch, op. cit., p.49.
22. "Torture in El Salvador", CDHES, San Salvador, September 1986.
23. *Central America Bulletin*, Berkeley, California, May 1986.
24. Thames TV, 14 January 1986.
25. Americas Watch, op. cit., p.56.
26. CDHES, op. cit.
27. *Guardian*, 7 August 1986.
28. *Sunday Times*, 15 December 1985.
29. Americas Watch, op. cit., p.137.
30. Ibid., pp.129–30.

Part Four: *The Silenced Majority (pp. 113–142)*

1. *El Salvador Briefing*, London, September 1986.
2. Ibid., March 1986.
3. *Inforpress Centroamericano*, 7 August 1986.
4. *El Salvador Briefing*, September 1986.
5. CINAS No. 20.
6. See Chapter 3.
7. "*El Salvador: The Struggle for Peace and Freedom*", the Report of the Labour Movement Delegation, London, 1986, p.16.
8. *El Salvador Briefing*, April 1986.
9. *Inforpress*, 8 May 1986, p.10.
10. *Central America Report* No. 28, London, May/June 1986, p.3 — some sources were said to claim that state employees were ordered to attend and that participants were paid between 50 and 75 *colones*.
11. *Inforpress*, 8 May 1986.
12. See Chapter 2.
13. Matheson, Catherine, "Left Urges Salvador Talks", *Guardian*, 30 September 1985.
14. See Chapter 1.
15. For example: "Universidad por la Paz", II Jornada, University of El Salvador, December 1985; "Foro Nacional por la Supervivencia y la Paz del Pueblo Salvadoreño", UNTS and FENAPES, April 1986, reported in *Estudios Centroamericanos*, May 1986; Inforpress, 4 September 1986, etc.
16. *Inforpress*, 4 September 1986.
17. *Proceso*, Central American University, June 1986.
18. *Inforpress*, 4 September 1986.
19. *Inforpress*, 7 August 1986.
20. *Inforpress*, 10 July 1986.
21. *Inforpress*, 11 September 1986.
22. See Chapter 10.
23. See "El Salvador Crunch Talks", *Guardian* Third World Review, 6 September 1986.
24. *Salpress*, Mexico City, 1–7 September 1986.

25. *Salpress*, 17–23 August 1986.
26. *Salpress*, 24–31 August 1986.
27. *Carta a las Iglesias*, UCA, San Salvador, 1–15 October 1986.
28. *Carta a las Iglesias*, 1–15 July 1986.
29. See Chapters 9 and 10.
30. *Settling Into Routine*, Human Rights Abuses in Duarte's Second Year, Americas Watch, New York, May 1986, p.79., also, see Chapter 6.
31. Americas Watch, op. cit., p.85.
32. *Inforpress Centroamericano*, 5 June 1986.
33. *El Salvador Briefing*, London, July 1986.
34. See Chapters 6 and 7.
35. Communicado de Prensa, 17 June 1986.
36. *Carta a las Iglesias*, 16–31 July 1986.
37. Ibid.
38. Shade, Raoul, "Eyewitness in El Salvador", *AfricAsia*, Paris, October 1986, p.47.
39. *Carta a las Iglesias*, op. cit.
40. Ibid.